PHOTOCOPIABLE MASTERS

Talk-A-Tivities

Problem Solving and Puzzles for Pairs

Richard Yorkey

Alta Book Center Publishers—San Francisco

14 Adrian Court, Burlingame, California 94010 USA

The Author

Richard Yorkey has taught English and trained teachers of English for Speakers of Other Languages at the American University of Beirut, Lebanon; Concordia University in Montreal; and St. Michael's College in Winooski, Vermont, where *Talk-A-Tivities* was developed and tested.

Illustrations: Richard Yorkey, Elizabeth Hazelton, and Larry Matteson
Cover Design: Bruce Marion Design
Text Design: Herb Caswell

Acknowledgements

Pages 58–59, reprinted with permission of *The Encyclopedia Americana*, copyright 1983, Grolier, Inc.

Pages 116–118 from Sears, Roebuck catalog, 1927, used by permission of Sears, Robuck and Co.

Pages 120–121 used by permission of Pan-American World Airways.

Alta Book Center Publishers
14 Adrian Court
Burlingame, California 94010 USA
Phone: 800 ALTA/ESL • 650.692.1285 (Int'l)
Fax: 800 ALTA/FAX • 650.692.4654 (Int'l)
Email: info@alteasl.com • Website: www.altaesl.com

ISBN: 1-882483-85-5

INTRODUCTION

Fostering Communication

Communication is a stated goal of most contemporary English language programs, but many teachers are unsure how to foster and develop it. Textbooks teach many essential skills; too often, however, students become familiar with the dialogues and situations in their texts but are unable to express their own thoughts and ideas—and their wants and needs—in real-life, day-to-day contacts. Conversation classes, while helpful, tend to share the limitations of the textbooks. How, then, can teachers help students develop real communicative competence?

There can be no single answer to such a question. One method, however, that has been unusually effective with many students is the use of structured puzzle and problem situations which can be solved only by the cooperation of two or more students. Restricted to the target language, students must create their own discourse with one another to complete the task or solve the problem.

Talk-A-Tivities is a collection of activities of this kind. Most of them are designed for completion by two students working cooperatively. With neither able to see the other's paper, students determine differences between pictures, follow routes on a map, track robbers through a maze of streets, reproduce line drawings, and solve a myriad of puzzles through verbal communication. As they work through the challenging but enjoyable activities, they practice communication and listening skills, sharpen their reasoning abilities, build their vocabularies, and deal with practical survival skills—making appointments, ordering from a catalog, using an international airline timetable, and so on.

Using the Activities

Talk-A-Tivities is produced in the form of reproducible blackline masters to provide for maximum flexibility and teacher control. You can choose which activities you wish to use at a particular time, produce the needed number (in most instances, one of each page per pair of students) and distribute them at the appropriate moment, after you have prepared the students for the activity and divided them into pairs (or groups for those activities for which this is suggested).

The activities should be chosen on the basis of student interests and needs and your own perception of areas that require review, reinforcement, or practice. The order in which they appear in the Table of Contents is arbitrary. Activities are classified by type, but one type is not necessarily easier or harder than another. Within types, some of the activities with several pages are arranged in approximate order of difficulty, and a statement to this effect appears on the instruction page for that activity.

If you plan to use all or most of the activities during the semester or year, you may wish to have them duplicated in advance—perhaps fifteen copies of each (or more or fewer depending on class size). The duplicated pages can be placed in manila folders or envelopes, making a kit of activities ready for use as needed. Note that pages 19, 46, 53, and 115 are response sheets for two or more other pages and that pages 2 through 4, 11, 61 through 69, and 93 through 95 are to be cut apart for use by several students.

Most of the activities are designed for pair use, some for small groups. You will probably want to change student pairing and small group composition from one activity to another so that students can get maximum practice in communicating with a variety of other persons. Be sure that the classroom is arranged to permit pairs of students to face each other and small groups to see and hear one another. If you have a language laboratory and individual stations can be "patched" together (as is true in many cases), some pair activity may be conducted with each partner at his or her own station, communicating by microphone and earphone with the other. This simulates the telephone conversation situation and would be especially appropriate with the "Appointment Book" activities (pages 28–37) and those using the mail order catalog (pages 115–117).

The instruction pages provide brief descriptions of the activities together with statements of their rationale and purpose. These are followed by step-by-step directions for using the activity and, where applicable, answer keys. You may wish to fill in answers on a duplicated copy for easy comparison with students' papers. Most of the activities, however, are self-correcting, in that students receive immediate feedback by comparing each other's papers.

I would like to thank my colleagues at the International Student Program at St. Michael's College who gave me valuable suggestions and reports during their trial of various activities. Their students and mine were willing and enthusiastic guinea pigs, and I am grateful. Some of my TESL graduate students at St. Michael's also offered helpful comments, and I'm especially pleased to acknowledge the insightful criticism of Mary Plante and Deryn Verity. Finally, I am happy to thank Talbot F. Hamlin and Elly Schottman for their unusual pedagogical perspective, their sensible suggestions, and their careful editing of a complicated collection of diverse activities.

Richard Yorkey

CONTENTS

Crosswords for Paired Practice _____

Buying by Mail _____

Flying Away _____

Lend Me Your Ears, like the other Listening Activities, provides practice in the skill of aural (listening) comprehension. *Lend Me Your Ears* may also be used as a communication or reading comprehension exercise (see options 2 and 3).

Lend Me Your Ears 1 deals with direction words: left, right, up, and down.
Lend Me Your Ears 2 deals with the past tenses of irregular verbs.
Lend Me Your Ears 3 deals with pronunciation of vowel and consonant sounds.

Procedure

Option 1 (Listening Comprehension)

a. Cut the directions from the bottom of the page.

b. Distribute the grid. Draw students' attention to the letters at the left and the numbers at the bottom. Explain that you will give them some oral directions. They are to listen carefully and do exactly as they are told. *Warn students that they will hear each direction only once.* (If you feel it would be useful, you may omit this warning and repeat the directions.)

c. Speak loudly and clearly enough to make this a fair test of aural comprehension. Pause about ten seconds after each direction. (This timing can be adjusted to the pace of the average student.)

d. At the end of the activity, read aloud the answers (below) and discuss with students where they might have gone wrong.

Option 2 (Communication)

a. Cut the directions from the bottom of the page.

b. Have students form pairs. Give the grid to one student (A) and the directions to the other student (B).

c. Without looking at each other's paper, B should tell A what to do. Draw B's attention to the letters at the left and the numbers at the bottom of the grid. Encourage students to use only English. Student A

may ask for repetition or clarification, but may not look at the direction.

d. When both partners are ready, they should review the directions together and agree on the answers. When all pairs have completed the activity, read the correct answers to the class and discuss with students where they might have gone wrong.

Option 3 (Reading Comprehension)

a. Leave the directions at the bottom of the page and distribute one copy of it to each student.

b. Draw students' attention to the letters at the left and the numbers at the bottom of the grid. Explain simply that they are to read and follow the directions exactly.

c. The time allowed for this activity may be set for the general proficiency of the class or adjusted to the individual speed of each student.

d. Give answers at the end so that students may check their accuracy and learn from their mistakes.

Answer Key

Lend Me Your Ears 1   1. B-2;   2. F-5;   3. H-9;   4. H-16;   5. C-14;   6. B-11;   7. G-7;   8. B-2
Lend Me Your Ears 2   X. E-9;   2. B-9;   3. E-12;   4. B-12;   5. H-6;   6. E-6;   7. H-9;   8. B-6;   9. H-12
Lend Me Your Ears 3   X. F-9;   2. H-9;   3. F-3;   4. I-9;   5. F-12;   6. G-9;   7. F-1;   8. J-9

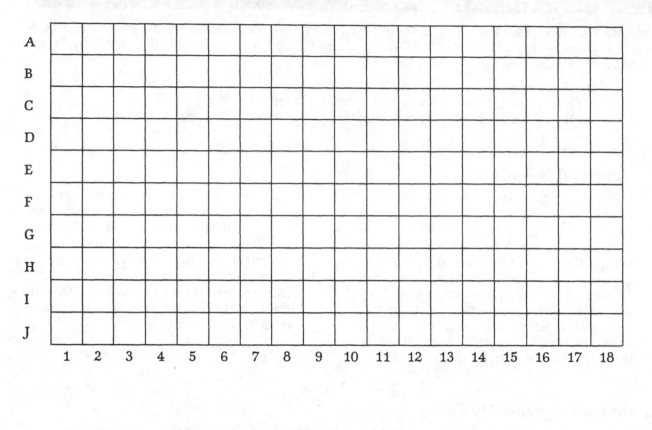

cut along dotted line

GIVE YOUR PARTNER THESE DIRECTIONS. THEN CHECK THE GRID FOR THE ACCURACY OF COMMUNICATION AND COMPREHENSION.

1. Start by putting the number 1 in the B-2 square.
2. Now go right 3 spaces and down 4 spaces. Put a 2 in the square.
3. From there, go right 4 spaces and down 2 spaces. Put a 3 in the square.
4. From there, go right 7 spaces and put a 4 in the square.
5. From there, go up 5 spaces and left 2 spaces. Put a 5 in the square.
6. Now go left 3 spaces and up 1 space. Put a 6 in the square.
7. Go left 4 spaces and down 5 spaces. Put a 7 in the square.
8. From there, go left 5 spaces and up 5 spaces. Put an 8 in that square. WHERE ARE YOU?

Talk-A-Tivities©2002 Alta Book Center Publishers, San Francisco, California
Permission granted to photocopy for one teacher's classroom use only.

LEND ME YOUR EARS (2)

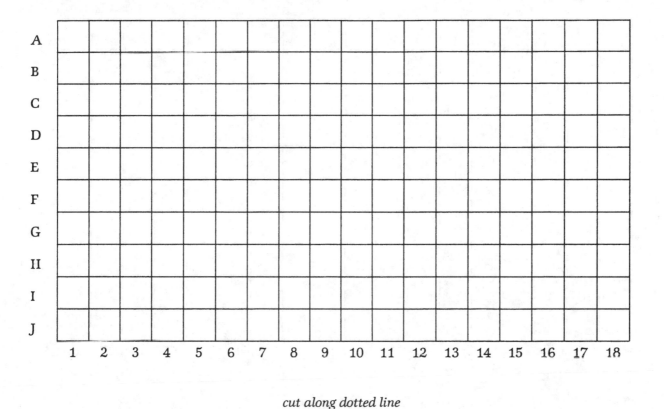

cut along dotted line

- -

1. Tell your partner to start by putting an X in the E-9 square.

   NOW USE THESE OR SIMILAR WORDS FOR ALL OF THE FOLLOWING DIRECTIONS.

2. If the past tense of GO is GONE, put the number 2 in C-5. However,
   if the past tense of GO is WENT, put 2 in B-9.

3. If the past tense of HIT is HIT, put a number 3 in E-12.
   If the past tense of HIT is HUT, put a number 3 in G-15.

4. If the past tense of SHOOT is SHOT, put 4 in B-12.
   If the past tense of SHOOT is SHUT, put 4 in J-3.

5. If the past tense of FLY is FLOW, put 5 in E-16.
   If the past tense of FLY is FLEW, put 5 in H-6.

6. If the past tense of FALL is FELL, put 6 in E-6.
   If the past tense of FALL is FULL, put 6 in A-4.

7. If the past tense of SLEEP is SLEPT, put 7 in H-9.
   If the past tense of SLEEP is SLAP, put 7 in F-2.

8. If the past tense of SWIM is SWUM, put 8 in I-10.
   If the past tense of SWIM is SWAM, put 8 in B-6.

9. If the past tense of SHAKE is SHOCK, put 9 in F-14.
   If the past tense of SHAKE is SHOOK, put 9 in H-12.

NOW CHECK THE LOCATION OF YOUR PARTNER'S NUMBERS. ARE THEY IN THE RIGHT SQUARES?

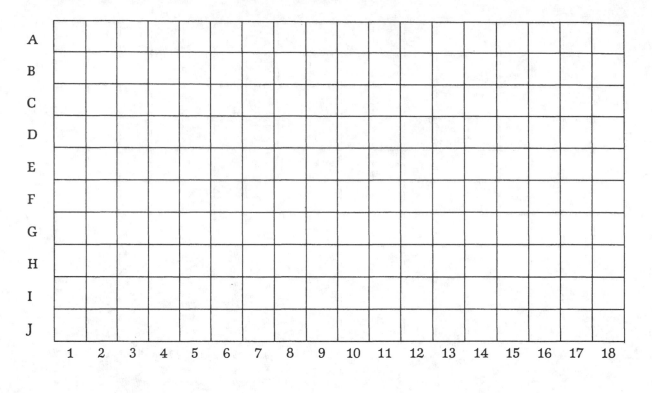

cut along dotted line

----

1. Tell your partner to start by putting an X in the F-9 square. *Each of the following directions will start from this square!*

   NOW USE THESE OR SIMILAR WORDS FOR ALL OF THE FOLLOWING DIRECTIONS.

2. If you would like to eat SOAP, go up 2 spaces from X and put 2 in the square.
   If you would like to eat SOUP, go down 2 spaces from X and put 2 in the square.

3. If you can write with a PEN, go left 6 spaces from X and put 3 in the square.
   If you can write with a PAIN, go right 6 spaces from X and put 3 in the square.

4. If you'd like to sit on GLASS, go up 4 spaces from X and put 4 in the square.
   If you'd like to sit on GRASS, go down 3 spaces from X and put 4 in the square.

5. If you'd like to wear a COAT, go right 3 spaces from X and put 5 in the square.
   If you'd like to wear a GOAT, go up 1 space from X and put 5 in the square.

6. If you eat with your MOUTH, go down 1 space from X and put 6 in the square.
   If you eat with your MOUSE, go left 3 spaces from X and put 6 in the square.

7. If an animal that barks and wags its tail is a DOG, go left 8 spaces from X and put 7 in the square. If it's a DUCK, go right 5 spaces from X and put 7 in the square.

8. If you'd like to go to Hawaii on a SHEEP, go up 3 spaces from X and put 8 in the square. If you'd prefer to go on a SHIP, go down 4 spaces from X and put 8 in the square.

THE UNICORN IN THE GARDEN and COPS AND ROBBERS / Instructions

In these two activities, one student directs another in following a route through a maze. The two students communicate only by speaking and may not look at each other's papers. Students will be using directional terms north, south, east, and west as well as cardinal and ordinal numbers.

Procedure

a. Distribute the page and have students form pairs.

b. Read the instructions at the bottom of the page. If students are unsure about such terms as *unicorn, cops,* and *robbers,* clarify the meanings. Call attention to the compass rose and be sure students understand its use. Tell them to use the direction words in doing the activity.

c. Student A is the unicorn (or the robber), and should trace a route through the maze with a pencil. He or she can make the route long or complicated, but it must be described clearly and accurately so Student B can follow the directions. (Note that the route cannot contain any diagonal lines.)

d. Student B is the pursuer (the hunter or cop). Student B learns about the unicorn's (or robber's) route by asking Student A to describe it. Student A must answer Student B's questions honestly. *Emphasize to the students that they may not look at each other's papers.*

e. At the end of the activity, students should compare their routes to determine the accuracy of their communication and comprehension.

A sample of student dialogue might be something like this:

B. Where did you come into the garden?

A. I came into the garden on the west side at the seventh square from the south edge of the garden.

B. Where did you go then?

A. I went three squares north, then six squares east.

B. Then what did you do?

A. Then I went two squares south.
   etc.

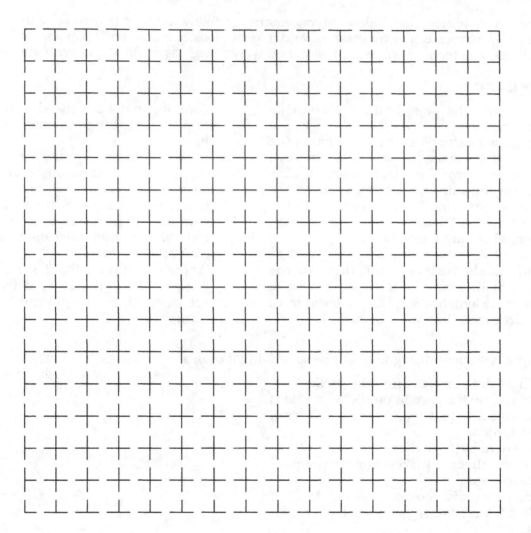

Talk-A-Tivities©2002 Alta Book Center Publishers, San Francisco, California
Permission granted to photocopy for one teacher's classroom use only.

READ DIRECTIONS FOR BOTH PARTNERS!

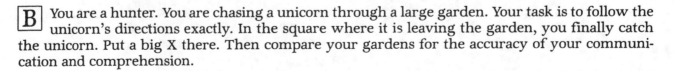

A You are a unicorn. You run into and out of a large garden because you are being chased by a hunter. On this grid, trace your path through the garden. Enter and exit anywhere you want, but you can go through only the open spaces. You cannot cross any black lines. Then be ready to describe your path to the hunter.

B You are a hunter. You are chasing a unicorn through a large garden. Your task is to follow the unicorn's directions exactly. In the square where it is leaving the garden, you finally catch the unicorn. Put a big X there. Then compare your gardens for the accuracy of your communication and comprehension.

COPS AND ROBBERS

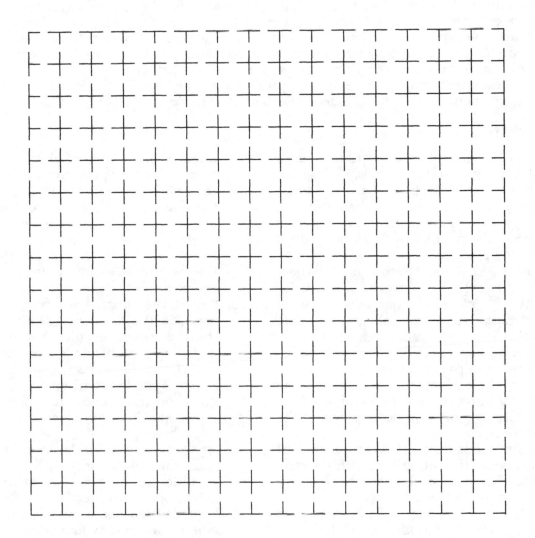

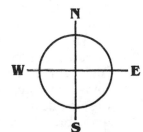

READ DIRECTIONS FOR BOTH PARTNERS

A You are a robber. You have just robbed a bank and are now driving
fast through the streets of the city. You are being chased by the
police. In any square of the city, put a circle to represent the bank. Then trace your route through
the city to the place where you leave the city. You can go through only the open spaces. You cannot cross any black line. Then be ready to describe your route to the cops.

B You are a cop. A robber has just robbed a bank and you are speeding your police car through
the city, chasing the robber's car. Your task is to start at the bank and follow the robber's
directions exactly. You finally catch the robber's car as it is leaving the city. Put a big X there.
Then compare your maps for the accuracy of your communication and comprehension.

Space Invaders requires four students. If you're working with a class, divide it into groups of four. Extra students (if the number in the class is not divisible by four) can serve as floating observers, silently watching and listening to several groups; later they can report on what they observed.

In *Space Invaders*, information about location is relayed from person to person, with each person recording it on a Galaxy Grid as he or she receives it, and then passing it on to the next person. All communication is in words: no person sees the others' grids.

The four students play the roles of the Space Invader, the First Spy (code name "B"), the Second Spy (code name "C"), and Intelligence Headquarters (code name "SpyChief").

Procedure

a. Set up the groups of four students each and pass out the Galaxy Grids. Each group member has a Grid. (If there are to be floating observers, explain their function and provide them with plain paper to record any problems that the groups seem to be having.)

b. "Set the scene" for the students. Tell them that this activity concerns an invader from outer space who has secretly placed five space ships in our galaxy. This Space Invader has sent a radio message to Invasion Headquarters telling them where the five space ships are located.

Tell the students that, fortunately, one of our Spies (code name B) was able to hear this message and now knows where the five ships are.

B is under instructions to transmit all information to another spy with the code name of C. So B tells C where the invading space ships are located.

C, in turn, sends this information to Intelligence Headquarters (called Spy-Chief).

c. Assign the roles (or have students volunteer for them). Space Invader places an X on the grid. This is home base. Space Invader then positions the five space ships that will carry out the invasion. Space Invader writes the numbers 1 through 5 in five different squares (anywhere on the grid, but preferably far enough apart so that if one is found the others will still be

safe). These numbers show where the space ships are. Space invader then "sends the radio message." (The student playing the role must decide how to describe the locations so that other students can accurately plot them.) *This message is to be heard only by Spy B.* (Within the group, this may most easily be done by having Space Invader whisper the message to B.)

d. B hears the message and marks on his or her grid the locations of the five space ships. B then transmits this message (in words only) to his or her contact, Spy C. *(Only C is to hear this transmission.)*

e. C marks the locations on his or her own grid, and then sends the information to SpyChief. *(Only SpyChief is to hear C's message.)*

f. SpyChief marks the location of the five space ships on his or her grid.

g. SpyChief captures the five space ships by telling Space Invader where each one is located. Each space ship is surrendered when it is correctly located.

h. If any of the space ships is not correctly located, SpyChief has to find out why. A check of the four grids will help to show who is responsible. The group members involved can decide (perhaps with the help of an observer) how the error occurred. Was it in transmission (speaking) or in reception (hearing and marking)?

To complicate the communication a bit, space ships might be different sizes: a Space Mini = 1 square, a Stellar Rocket = 2 squares, and a Cosmos Cruiser = 3 squares. Accurate communication will indicate what kind of ship is involved and describe its entire location.

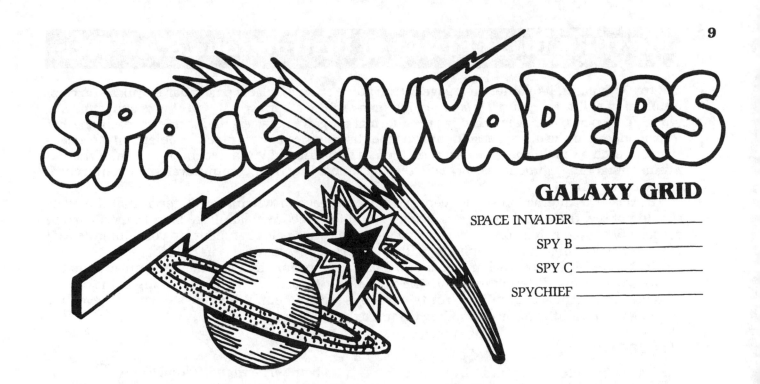

GALAXY GRID

SPACE INVADER _____

SPY B _____

SPY C _____

SPYCHIEF _____

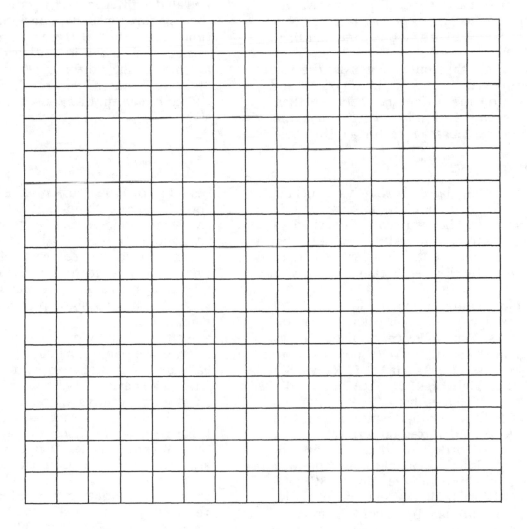

Picture Differences, like other Language Interaction Activities, places particular emphasis on communication skills. In *Picture Differences* and many of the other activities in this group, students, working in pairs, discover there is an "information gap" between them; that is, each one has information that the other doesn't, information that is necessary to solve a problem, make a decision, or reach a conclusion. In every case, there is some kind of visual feedback so that, if there is misunderstanding, students can actually see where and why their communication or comprehension went wrong.

Because the interaction is between two students, each of whom has material that the other should not see, these activities are especially useful for practice in language labs. In most current consoles, a simple patch cord between two inputs allows a pair of students to communicate as if they were speaking on the telephone, without interfering with others in the lab.

In *Picture Differences* each member of the pair has a picture that is generally similar to that of his/her partner but different in detail. The challenge is to discover, without looking at the other's picture, the specific ways in which the two pictures are different. When the students believe they have identified all the differences, they compare their pictures.

Procedure

a. Have students form pairs. Give one partner the A picture of a particular set. Give the other partner the B picture. *Neither partner is to see the other's picture.* (Note that 1A and 1B are on one page. Cut them apart.)

b. Communicating only in words, the two partners describe their pictures and decide on the differences between them by asking and answering questions. When partners agree on a difference, both write that difference down.

c. When partners believe they have identified all the differences, they then compare their pictures visually, checking to see if there are other differences that they missed, or if some identified differences are not, in fact, differences at all. (Such "false differences" can result from difficulties in communication or comprehension.)

Answer Key

1. a. no glasses, glasses; b. short vs. long hair; c. smiling, frowning; d. bow vs. long tie; e. black vs. checked coat; f. checked vs. white pants; g. umbrella in right vs. left hand; h. suitcase in left vs. right hand; i. white vs. black shoes; j. Hawaii vs. Alaska label on suitcase.

2. a. man's hair color; b. no glasses vs. glasses; c. woman's hair color; d. War *and* Peace vs. War *or* Peace; e. dictionary vs. English book; f. no notebook vs. notebook; g. left bookshelf HISTORY vs. SCIENCE; h. right shelf BIOGRAPHY vs. HISTORY; i. calendar FEBRUARY vs. OCTOBER; j. calendar house on right vs. left; k. calendar tree on left vs. right; l. Sign word order; m. double doors and two windows vs. single door and window; n. sign above door, SCHOOL LIBRARY vs. LIBRARY; o. shape of clock.

3. a. flag vs. no flag; b. no curtains in closed window vs. curtains in open window; c. three vs. two top windows in corner building; d. Hal's Barber vs. Al's Beauty Shop; e. shop door in center vs. right; f. two shop windows vs. one; g. barber pole vs. none; h. apples, 89¢ lb. vs. eggs, 89¢ dozen; i. price of ice cream; j. time on clock; k. temperature; l. direction of one-way sign; m. Parking vs. Bank; n. Bank vs. Hotel; o. bus sign; p. bus company name.

4. a. woman's hair color; b. woman's jacket color; c. woman's skirt color; d. no purse vs. purse; e. age of man; f. man thin vs. fat; g. man dark hair vs. bald; h. no glasses vs. glasses; i. coat vs. no coat; j. striped tie vs. polka dot; k. no briefcase vs. briefcase; l. dark vs. white shoes; m. sign: Danger Men Working vs. Men Danger at Work; n. sign on sawhorse vs. post; o. graffiti: $2+2=4$ vs. $2+2=5$; p. teacher happy female vs. sad male; q. tic-tac-toe: X and O reversed; r. heart = JW vs. WJ; s. Billy loves Mary vs. Mary loves Billy; t. two vs. three trees; u. School vs. Factory.

PICTURE DIFFERENCES 1B

Talk-A-Tivities©2002 Alta Book Center Publishers, San Francisco, California
Permission granted to photocopy for one teacher's classroom use only.

PICTURE DIFFERENCES 1A

PICTURE DIFFERENCES 2A

Talk-A-Tivities©2002 Alta Book Center Publishers, San Francisco, California
Permission granted to photocopy for one teacher's classroom use only.

PICTURE DIFFERENCES 2B

PICTURE DIFFERENCES 3A

14

PICTURE DIFFERENCES 3B

PICTURE DIFFERENCES 4A

PICTURE DIFFERENCES 4B

PICTURE THAT! / Instructions

For this activity, students work together in pairs. Student A is given a picture to describe to Student B. Student B draws the picture from Student A's description. The challenge for A is to describe the picture accurately enough for B to reproduce it. The challenge for B is to comprehend the description well enough to draw a reasonable facsimile of the original. The accuracy of their communication and comprehension is immediately verified by comparing Student B's drawing with the original picture. The pedagogical advantage of this immediate feedback is complemented by the amusement of the students as they compare the artistic accomplishments of the various class members.

Procedure

a. Have students form pairs. Describe the task: one member of the pair will have a picture and will describe this picture to the other member; the other member will draw the picture from the first member's description. *Emphasize that neither member can look at the other's paper until the exercise is completed.*

b. Pass out copies of the selected picture to one member of each group. Pass out blank forms to the other member. Ask the students to read the instructions on the page. Point out that the partner who is describing the Picture (Student A) should first describe the entire scene as a whole and then describe each part. The partner who is drawing (Student B) can ask questions if Student A's description is not clear. Then have the students do the exercise.

c. When all the drawings are complete, partners can compare the reproduced picture with the original and discuss differences.

PICTURE THAT!

Your partner will describe a simple line drawing to you. Do not look at the picture; just listen! As your partner describes it to you, draw the picture in the frame below.

If your partner's directions do not seem clear, ask questions. Your purpose is to make your picture as much as possible like the one being described to you.

When you have drawn your picture, look at the original picture. Compare the two of them and discuss any differences with your partner.

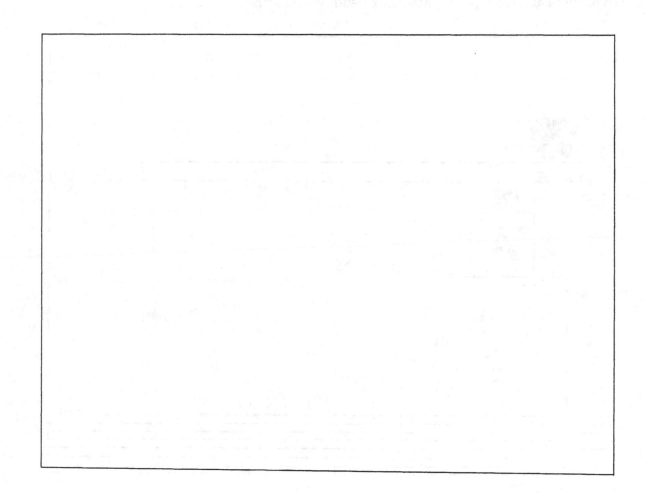

PICTURE THAT! (1)

You will describe this drawing to your partner. *Do not show the drawing to your partner.* Just describe it. Your partner will try to draw a copy of the picture from your description of it, so be as clear and complete as you can.

If your directions do not seem clear, your partner may ask you questions. Answer them clearly and completely. Try to help your partner to make a drawing as much as possible like the one you are describing.

When your partner has drawn the picture, show him or her the one on this page. Compare the two of them and discuss any differences with your partner.

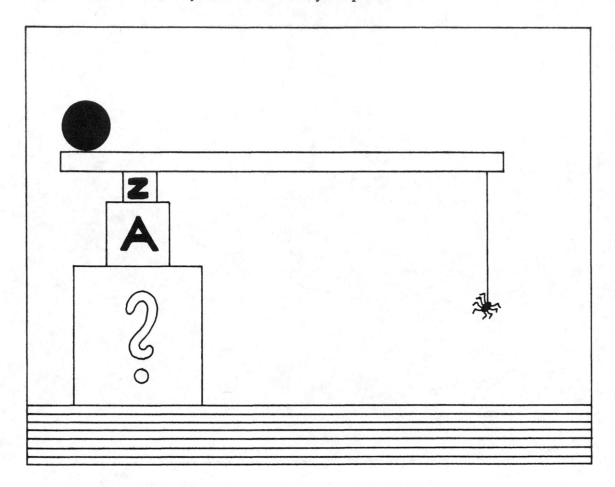

PICTURE THAT! (2)

You will describe this drawing to your partner. *Do not show the drawing to your partner.* Just describe it. Your partner will try to draw a copy of the picture from your description of it, so be as clear and complete as you can.

If your directions do not seem clear, your partner may ask you questions. Answer them clearly and completely. Try to help your partner to make a drawing as much as possible like the one you are describing.

When your partner has drawn the picture, show him or her the one on this page. Compare the two of them and discuss any differences with your partner.

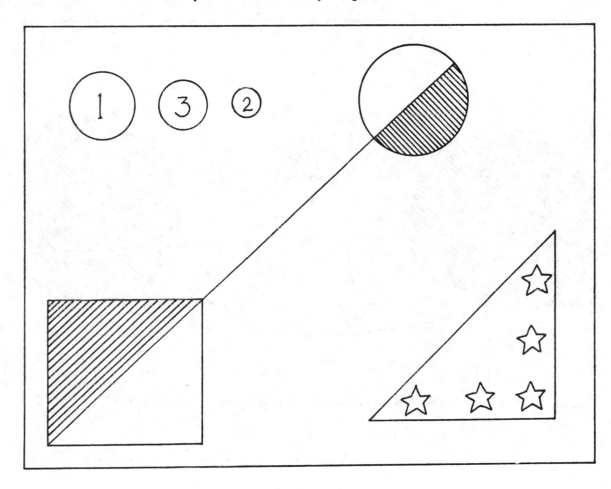

PICTURE THAT! (3)

You will describe this drawing to your partner. *Do not show the drawing to your partner.* Just describe it. Your partner will try to draw a copy of the picture from your description of it, so be as clear and complete as you can.

If your directions do not seem clear, your partner may ask you questions. Answer them clearly and completely. Try to help your partner to make a drawing as much as possible like the one you are describing.

When your partner has drawn the picture, show him or her the one on this page. Compare the two of them and discuss any differences with your partner.

Talk-A-Tivities©2002 Alta Book Center Publishers, San Francisco, California
Permission granted to photocopy for one teacher's classroom use only.

PICTURE THAT! (4)

You will describe this drawing to your partner. *Do not show the drawing to your partner.* Just describe it. Your partner will try to draw a copy of the picture from your description of it, so be as clear and complete as you can.

If your directions do not seem clear, your partner may ask you questions. Answer them clearly and completely. Try to help your partner to make a drawing as much as possible like the one you are describing.

When your partner has drawn the picture, show him or her the one on this page. Compare the two of them and discuss any differences with your partner.

PICTURE THAT! (5)

You will describe this drawing to your partner. *Do not show the drawing to your partner.* Just describe it. Your partner will try to draw a copy of the picture from your description of it, so be as clear and complete as you can.

If your directions do not seem clear, your partner may ask you questions. Answer them clearly and completely. Try to help your partner to make a drawing as much as possible like the one you are describing.

When your partner has drawn the picture, show him or her the one on this page. Compare the two of them and discuss any differences with your partner.

Talk-A-Tivities©2002 Alta Book Center Publishers, San Francisco, California
Permission granted to photocopy for one teacher's classroom use only.

PICTURE THAT! (6)

You will describe this drawing to your partner. *Do not show the drawing to your partner.* Just describe it. Your partner will try to draw a copy of the picture from your description of it, so be as clear and complete as you can.

If your directions do not seem clear, your partner may ask you questions. Answer them clearly and completely. Try to help your partner to make a drawing as much as possible like the one you are describing.

When your partner has drawn the picture, show him or her the one on this page. Compare the two of them and discuss any differences with your partner.

PICTURE THAT! (7)

You will describe this drawing to your partner. *Do not show the drawing to your partner.* Just describe it. Your partner will try to draw a copy of the picture from your description of it, so be as clear and complete as you can.

If your directions do not seem clear, your partner may ask you questions. Answer them clearly and completely. Try to help your partner to make a drawing as much as possible like the one you are describing.

When your partner has drawn the picture, show him or her the one on this page. Compare the two of them and discuss any differences with your partner.

Talk-A-Tivities©2002 Alta Book Center Publishers, San Francisco, California
Permission granted to photocopy for one teacher's classroom use only.

Like the *Picture That!* activities, *The Appointment Book* provides interaction that is structured by its context. The context in this case is the real-life one of making appointments. Working again in pairs, students A and B are each given a page from an appointment book. Each plays the role of a particular character and interacts with the other to reach agreement on a mutually convenient time to meet.

If you are using this activity with low-intermediate students, it may be helpful to introduce or review some of the commonly used conventional expressions for this kind of interchange. For example:

Requesting an Appointment	May I meet you at . . . ? Could I see you at . . . Is Friday at 9:00 possible?	Would 9:30 be all right? What about . . . ? How about . . . ?

Rejecting an Appointment	I'm sorry, but 9:00 is
	    impossible.
		I can't make it then.
		No, that's not a good time
		    (either).

Making a Counter-Proposal	Would 10:00 be possible?
	I suggest 11:00. Is that
	    convenient for you?
		I'm free at 2:00. Could you
		    make it then?
		Well, how/what about 3:00?

Procedure

a. Tell the students that this exercise will give them practice in making appointments. Each will have a copy of a page from an appointment book showing his or her appointments for five days. The students will work in pairs. One member of each pair will try to arrange an appointment with the other member. Each will be able to see only his or her own appointment book page, so the two members of the pair will have to talk back and forth to work out a time and date that is mutually satisfactory.

b. Distribute copies of the selected appointment book pages. Be sure that one of the pair members has the A sheet and the other has the associated B sheet. *Pair members may not see each other's pages.* They can communicate only verbally. If a language lab is available and pairs of students can be patched together, the illusion of trying to work out an appointment by telephone will be enhanced.

c. Have students read the instructions at the top of the page. Answer any questions they may have about the situations presented. Tell them they can schedule an appointment only at a time when nothing else is scheduled.

d. Give each student an opportunity to play both an "A" role (person requesting an appointment) and a "B" role (person with whom an appointment is being requested). A student's "A" and "B" roles should be in different situations (for example, 1A and 2B or 3A and 1B). This gives each student practice in initiating a request.

e. After the exercise is completed, discuss with the class any difficulties they encountered.

You are an ESL student. You are unhappy about the grade on your last composition. You think it is better than the D which your teacher marked it. Ask for an appointment with your teacher to talk about it.

1A

MONDAY	MONDAY	MONDAY	MONDAY	MONDAY	MONDAY	MONDAY

9:00	reading class	1:00	pronunciation class
10:00	grammar class	2:00	writing class
11:00		3:00	language lab
12:00	lunch	4:00	

TUESDAY	TUESDAY	TUESDAY	TUESDAY	TUESDAY	TUESDAY	TUESD

9:00	reading class	1:00	
10:00	grammar class	2:00	writing class
11:00	language lab	3:00	conversation
12:00	lunch	4:00	

WEDNESDAY	WEDNESDAY	WEDNESDAY	WEDNESDAY	WEDNESDAY	WEDNESD

9:00	reading class	1:00	pronunciation class
10:00	grammar class	2:00	writing class
11:00		3:00	language lab
12:00	lunch	4:00	

THURSDAY	THURSDAY	THURSDAY	THURSDAY	THURSDAY	THURSDAY

9:00	reading class	1:00	
10:00	grammar class	2:00	writing class
11:00	language lab	3:00	conversation
12:00	lunch	4:00	

FRIDAY	FRIDAY	FRIDAY	FRIDAY	FRIDAY	FRIDAY	FRIDAY

9:00	reading class	1:00	pronunciation class
10:00	grammar class	2:00	writing class
11:00		3:00	language lab
12:00	lunch	4:00	

Talk-A-Trivities©2002 Alta Book Center Publishers, San Francisco, California
Permission granted to photocopy for one teacher's classroom use only.

1B

You are a teacher. One of your students is unhappy about the grade you assigned to a composition. The student will ask for an appointment with you to talk about the composition grade. Agree to meet the student at a time when both of you are free.

MONDAY MONDAY MONDAY MONDAY MONDAY MONDAY MONDAY

9:00	1:00
10:00	2:00 *writing class (level 6)*
11:00 *writing class (level 8)*	3:00
12:00	4:00 *take children shopping*

TUESDAY TUESDAY TUESDAY TUESDAY TUESDAY TUESDAY TUESD

9:00	1:00 *writing class (level 7)*
10:00	2:00 *writing class (level 6)*
11:00 *writing class (level 8)*	3:00
12:00	4:00 *language lab (level 3)*

WEDNESDAY WEDNESDAY WEDNESDAY WEDNESDAY WEDNESDAY WEDNESDA

9:00	1:00
10:00	2:00 *writing class (level 6)*
11:00 *writing class (level 8)*	3:00
12:00	4:00

THURSDAY THURSDAY THURSDAY THURSDAY THURSDAY THURSDAY

9:00	1:00 *writing class (level 7)*
10:00	2:00 *writing class (level 6)*
11:00 *writing class (level 8)*	3:00
12:00	4:00 *language lab (level 3)*

FRIDAY FRIDAY FRIDAY FRIDAY FRIDAY FRIDAY FRIDAY

9:00	1:00
10:00	2:00 *writing class (level 6)*
11:00 *writing class (level 8)*	3:00
12:00	4:00 *T.G.I.F. party*

You are a university student studying American History. You have lost interest in this field, especially after working on a farm last summer. Now you think you would like to be a farmer or a forest ranger. Ask for an appointment with the Career Guidance Officer to discuss your future.

2A

MONDAY	MONDAY	MONDAY	MONDAY	MONDAY	MONDAY	MONDAY
9:00	Political Science 243		1:00			
10:00			2:00	Political Science 308		
11:00	European History 219		3:00			
12:00			4:00	Work as cashier at Campus Grill.		

ESDAY	TUESDAY	TUESDAY	TUESDAY	TUESDAY	TUESDAY	TUESD
9:00	Philosophy 101		1:00			
10:00			2:00			
11:00			3:00			
12:00	English 217		4:00	Work as cashier at Campus Grill.		

DAY	WEDNESDAY	WEDNESDAY	WEDNESDAY	WEDNESDAY	WEDNESDA
9:00	Political Science 243		1:00		
10:00			2:00	Political Science 308	
11:00	European History 219		3:00		
12:00			4:00	Work as cashier at Campus Grill.	

RSDAY	THURSDAY	THURSDAY	THURSDAY	THURSDAY	THURSDAY
9:00	Philosophy 101		1:00		
10:00			2:00		
11:00			3:00		
12:00	English 217		4:00	Work as cashier at Campus Grill.	

FRIDAY	FRIDAY	FRIDAY	FRIDAY	FRIDAY	FRIDAY	FRIDAY
9:00	Political Science 243		1:00			
10:00			2:00	Political Science 308		
11:00	European History 219		3:00			
12:00			4:00	Work as cashier at Campus Grill.		

Talk-A-Tivities©2002 Alta Book Center Publishers, San Francisco, California
Permission granted to photocopy for one teacher's classroom use only.

You are a career guidance officer at a large university. A student wants to make an appointment with you, to discuss his or her interest in becoming either a farmer or a forest ranger, instead of a historian as planned. Agree to meet the student at a time that is convenient to both of you.

2B

MONDAY

9:00	1:00 Appointment: Mary Wilson
10:00 Appointment: Reiko Nakamura	2:00
11:00	3:00 } Shopping: special clothing
12:00 Lunch with the Dean	4:00 } sale at Shopper's World

TUESDAY

9:00	1:00 } Career Employment Opportunities
10:00 Appointment: Luis Morillo	2:00 } Conference at Rainbow Inn
11:00 Appointment: Ahmad Hasan'Id	3:00 } (West Vermillion Room)
12:00	4:00

WEDNESDAY

9:00	1:00 Lunch at Faculty Club
10:00 Appointment: Maria Gonzalez	2:00
11:00	3:00 Meeting with librarian
12:00 Lunch at Faculty Club	4:00

THURSDAY

9:00	1:00 } Guidance Office Weekly
10:00 meeting with Computybyte Representative	2:00 } Staff meeting
11:00 Appointment: George Klavitski	3:00 Appointment: Thu Trinh
12:00	4:00

FRIDAY

9:00	1:00 Appointment: Robert Sink
10:00 Appointment: Sylvia Beaulieu	2:00
11:00	3:00
12:00 Lunch at Macdougall's	4:00

You are an accountant in a large office. You have worked in the same position for nine years and think it's time for either a raise in pay or promotion to a higher position. Make an appointment with your boss to discuss your desire for a raise or promotion.

MONDAY	MONDAY	MONDAY	MONDAY	MONDAY	MONDAY	MONDAY
9:00			1:00 *Gonzalez account*			
10:00			2:00 *Gonzalez account*			
11:00 *Meeting with lawyer for the Jones account*			3:00			
12:00 *Lunch*			4:00			

TUESDAY	TUESDAY	TUESDAY	TUESDAY	TUESDAY	TUESDAY	TUESDAY
9:00			1:00			
10:00			2:00 *Meeting with IRS*			
11:00			3:00			
12:00 *Lunch*			4:00			

WEDNESDAY	WEDNESDAY	WEDNESDAY	WEDNESDAY	WEDNESDAY	WEDNESDAY
9:00			1:00		
10:00 *Long-Life Insurance Co.*			2:00		
11:00			3:00 *Sleepy Pajamas Mfg. Co.*		
12:00 *Lunch*			4:00 *Accounting Division staff meeting*		

THURSDAY	THURSDAY	THURSDAY	THURSDAY	THURSDAY	THURSDAY
9:00 *Bernstein's account*			1:00		
10:00			2:00		
11:00			3:00 *Appointment with dentist*		
12:00 *Lunch*			4:00 *Appointment with dentist*		

FRIDAY	FRIDAY	FRIDAY	FRIDAY	FRIDAY	FRIDAY	FRIDAY
9:00 *Keller & Keller tax audit*			1:00			
10:00 *Keller & Keller tax audit*			2:00			
11:00			3:00			
12:00 *Lunch*			4:00			

You are the office manager of a large company. One of the accountants is unhappy that he or she has not been promoted or given a raise in nine years. The accountant wants to make an appointment to discuss this matter with you. Agree to meet at a time when both of you are free.

3B

MONDAY	MONDAY	MONDAY	MONDAY	MONDAY	MONDAY	MONDAY

9:00 Budget Committee	1:00
10:00 " "	2:00
11:00	3:00 Executive Meeting
12:00	4:00 " "

TUESDAY	TUESDAY	TUESDAY	TUESDAY	TUESDAY	TUESDAY	TUESD

9:00 Conference	1:00 Lunch with secretary
10:00 "	2:00
11:00 "	3:00 ABC meeting
12:00	4:00 Meet Sonny's school teacher

WEDNESDAY	WEDNESDAY	WEDNESDAY	WEDNESDAY	WEDNESDAY	WEDNESDA

9:00 NO APPOINTMENTS (Meditation)	1:00 Lunch with Board of Directors
10:00	2:00 " " " "
11:00 International Marketing a/c	3:00
12:00	4:00

THURSDAY	THURSDAY	THURSDAY	THURSDAY	THURSDAY	THURSDAY

9:00	1:00 Meet Ed + Joe for lunch
10:00) Meeting of Banking Committee	2:00 Newspaper Interview
11:00 } and Trust Officers	3:00
12:00	4:00

FRIDAY	FRIDAY	FRIDAY	FRIDAY	FRIDAY	FRIDAY	FRIDAY

9:00	1:00 Golf
10:00	2:00 "
11:00	3:00 "
12:00	4:00 "

You were hurt in an accident and want to sue the other driver. Ask for an appointment with a lawyer from Martin, Barton, and Jones. You are free only at the following times.

MONDAY MONDAY MONDAY MONDAY MONDAY MONDAY MONDAY			
9:00		1:00	*Lunch with friends*
10:00	*Meeting with boss*	2:00	
11:00		3:00	*Attend Little League Baseball*
12:00		4:00	*Game (Junior is pitching!)*

TUESDAY TUESDAY TUESDAY TUESDAY TUESDAY TUESDAY TUESD			
9:00		1:00	
10:00		2:00	*Staff meeting*
11:00		3:00	
12:00	*Appointment with dentist*	4:00	

WEDNESDAY WEDNESDAY WEDNESDAY WEDNESDAY WEDNESDA			
9:00		1:00	
10:00		2:00	
11:00		3:00	
12:00	*Lunch with friends*	4:00	*appointment to discuss summer camp for the children*

THURSDAY THURSDAY THURSDAY THURSDAY THURSDAY			
9:00	*talk to Junior's teacher about his behavior in class*	1:00	
10:00		2:00	
11:00		3:00	*Visit grandmother in Senior*
12:00		4:00	*Citizens Retirement Home*

FRIDAY FRIDAY FRIDAY FRIDAY FRIDAY FRIDAY FRIDAY			
9:00	*Renew driver's license*	1:00	
10:00	*and motor vehicle inspection*	2:00	*Staff meeting*
11:00		3:00	
12:00		4:00	

4B

You are a lawyer at Martin, Barton, and Jones—a law firm that specializes in accident cases. A client will ask you for an appointment. Find a time that is convenient to both of you.

MONDAY	MONDAY	MONDAY	MONDAY	MONDAY	MONDAY	MONDAY

9:00 Appointment: Hedda Fall		1:00
10:00		2:00 Appointment: Charles Walker
11:00 Appointment: J. B. Driver		3:00
12:00 Lunch		4:00

TUESDAY	TUESDAY	TUESDAY	TUESDAY	TUESDAY	TUESDAY	TUESDAY

9:00 Appointment: Armen Hokhanian		1:00 Lunch with Martin
10:00 Martin, Barton, and Jones		2:00
11:00 Board of Trustees Meeting		3:00 Golf at Country Club with
12:00		4:00 Emory Evergreen

WEDNESDAY	WEDNESDAY	WEDNESDAY	WEDNESDAY	WEDNESDAY	WEDNESDAY

9:00 Appointment: Gene Trigger		1:00 Lunch with Barton
10:00 Appointment: Gladys Prescott		2:00 Consultation with clerk at
11:00 Appointment: Justin Case		3:00 State University Law Library
12:00		4:00

THURSDAY	THURSDAY	THURSDAY	THURSDAY	THURSDAY	THURSDAY

9:00		1:00 Lunch with Jones
10:00		2:00 Appointment: June Day
11:00 Appointment: Lawyer for Caretaker Insurance		3:00
12:00 Appointment: Barry Hertz		4:00

FRIDAY	FRIDAY	FRIDAY	FRIDAY	FRIDAY	FRIDAY	FRIDAY

9:00		1:00 Lunch with Martin, Barton, and Jones
10:00		2:00
11:00 Appointment: David Fell		3:00 Prepare for case before
12:00 Appointment: E. Z. Rider		4:00 Supreme Court on Monday

You are a student at State University. Because of no fault of your own, you and your roommates have been told to leave your apartment off-campus. A newspaper advertisement has described an apartment that you may want to rent. Telephone the landlord and make an appointment to see the apartment.

5A

MONDAY MONDAY MONDAY MONDAY	MONDAY MONDAY MONDAY
9:00 English 104	1:00
10:00	2:00 Chemistry 115
11:00 Math 206	3:00
12:00	4:00 Soccer practice

TUESDAY TUESDAY TUESDAY TUESDAY	TUESDAY TUESDAY TUESDAY
9:00	1:00
10:00 Sociology 101	2:00 Physics Lab
11:00 Physics 111	3:00 Physics Lab
12:00	4:00 Soccer practice

WEDNESDAY WEDNESDAY WEDNESDAY	WEDNESDAY WEDNESDAY WEDNESDAY
9:00 English 104	1:00
10:00	2:00 Chemistry 115
11:00 Math 206	3:00
12:00 Lunch with professor	4:00 Soccer practice

THURSDAY THURSDAY THURSDAY	THURSDAY THURSDAY THURSDAY
9:00	1:00
10:00 Sociology 101	2:00 Chemistry Lab
11:00 Physics 111	3:00 Chemistry Lab
12:00	4:00 Soccer practice

FRIDAY FRIDAY FRIDAY FRIDAY	FRIDAY FRIDAY FRIDAY
9:00 English 104	1:00
10:00	2:00 Chemistry 115
11:00 Math 206	3:00
12:00	4:00 Soccer practice

Talk-A-Tivities©2002 Alta Book Center Publishers, San Francisco, California
Permission granted to photocopy for one teacher's classroom use only.

You own a building with several apartments near the campus of State University. One of your apartments is now vacant. A student will telephone you in order to make an appointment to see the apartment. Agree on a mutually convenient time to show the apartment.

5B

MONDAY	MONDAY	MONDAY	MONDAY	MONDAY	MONDAY	MONDAY
9:00			1:00 *Special Sale at Kiddie Korner*			
10:00 *Doctor's appointment*			2:00			
11:00			3:00 *Appointment with plumber*			
12:00 *Meet tenants from Apt. 4-C*			4:00			

TUESDAY	TUESDAY	TUESDAY	TUESDAY	TUESDAY	TUESDAY	TUESD
9:00 *Appointment with lawyer*			1:00 *My birthday: special luncheon*			
10:00			2:00			
11:00			3:00			
12:00 *My birthday: special luncheon*			4:00			

WEDNESDAY	WEDNESDAY	WEDNESDAY	WEDNESDAY	WEDNESDAY	WEDNESDA
9:00		1:00 *Library; return overdue book*			
10:00 *Meet with insurance agent*		2:00			
11:00		3:00 *Mrs. McGillicudy complaints*			
12:00		4:00			

THURSDAY	THURSDAY	THURSDAY	THURSDAY	THURSDAY	THURSDAY
9:00 *Appointment with tax lawyer*			1:00		
10:00			2:00		
11:00			3:00 *Visit mother-in-law*		
12:00 *Meet tenants from Apt. 4-C*			4:00		

FRIDAY	FRIDAY	FRIDAY	FRIDAY	FRIDAY	FRIDAY	FRIDAY
9:00			1:00 *Lunch with Wilhelmina*			
10:00 *State Bank (loan officer)*			2:00			
11:00			3:00 *Take driver's test*			
12:00 *Lunch with Wilhelmina*			4:00 *Take driver's test*			

This activity, and the several that follow it, all deal with using and understanding the language of location and direction. Students work in pairs. Student A has a diagram or map. Student B wants to know where something is or how to get to a particular place. Communicating with each other verbally, without looking at each other's papers, the partners interact until B marks the location on his or her diagram or map. The accuracy of the communication is immediately confirmed by comparing the two papers. This feedback presents the students with immediate reinforcement.

If you are using this activity with low-intermediate students, review vocabulary that they may need. For example:

Asking for Location	Where is *Treasure Island?* Where is the dictionary located?	Where can I find a book about 19th century art?
Giving Location	It's on the first/second/ fifth shelf. It's lying flat on the middle/bottom shelf.	It's in the left hand bookcase. It's (right) next to . . . . It's the fourth book from the right/left.

Procedure

a. Tell the students that this activity will help them to tell other people how to find books in the library. It will also help them to follow the directions of others who tell them where a particular book can be found.

b. Divide the class into pairs and distribute copies of *The Library 1A* and *B*. Be sure that one of the pair members has the A page and the other has the B page. *Pair members may not see each other's pages.* They can communicate only verbally.

c. Tell students that they are to describe the location of certain books and shelves to their partners. The locations of the books are shown on their page by numbers and there is a key to the numbers at the bottom of the page.

d. As Student A tells Student B where particular books are located, Student B writes the numbers of these books on his or her diagram (labeled *The Library 1B)*. (Note that number 6 is a shelf, not a book.)

e. When Student B has marked the numbers 1 to 8 on the diagram, he or she then describes the location of a second group of books to Student A, who writes the numbers of these on his or her diagram. (Note that number 14 is a shelf, not a book.)

f. More practice can be given with *The Library 2A* and *B*. (Note that numbers 2 and 11 are shelves, not books.)

g. When students have completed the activity, have them discuss any problems they may have encountered; ask how other students solved these problems.

h. If possible, recreate the situation using real books on shelves in the classroom, or ask students to go into the library and practice the same kind of exercise. For example, Student A might choose a book and then describe its location: "Tell me the name of the fourth book from the left on the bottom shelf of the left hand bookcase." Student B must locate the book and tell its title to Student A. Student B can then choose a book and go through the same exercise.

THE LIBRARY 1A

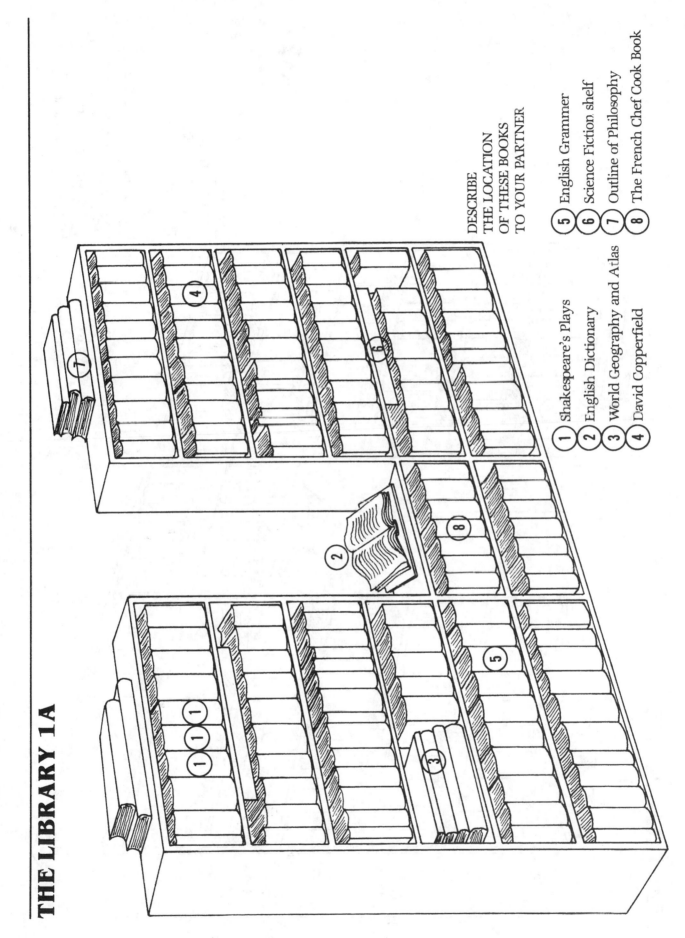

DESCRIBE
THE LOCATION
OF THESE BOOKS
TO YOUR PARTNER

1 Shakespeare's Plays
2 English Dictionary
3 World Geography and Atlas
4 David Copperfield
5 English Grammer
6 Science Fiction shelf
7 Outline of Philosophy
8 The French Chef Cook Book

THE LIBRARY 1B

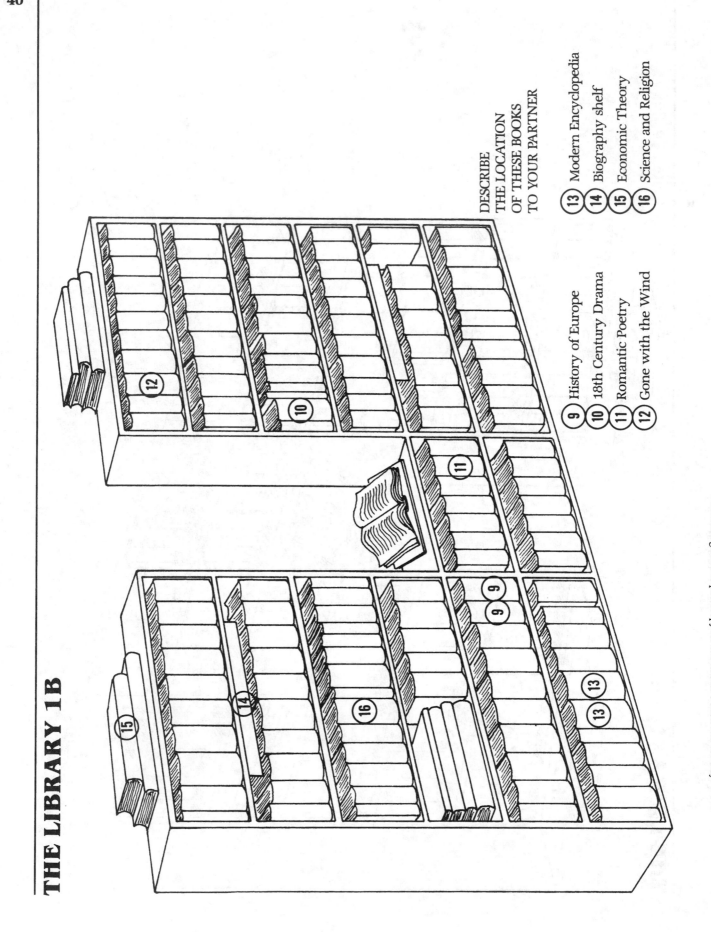

DESCRIBE
THE LOCATION
OF THESE BOOKS
TO YOUR PARTNER

9 History of Europe
10 18th Century Drama
11 Romantic Poetry
12 Gone with the Wind

13 Modern Encyclopedia
14 Biography shelf
15 Economic Theory
16 Science and Religion

THE LIBRARY 2A

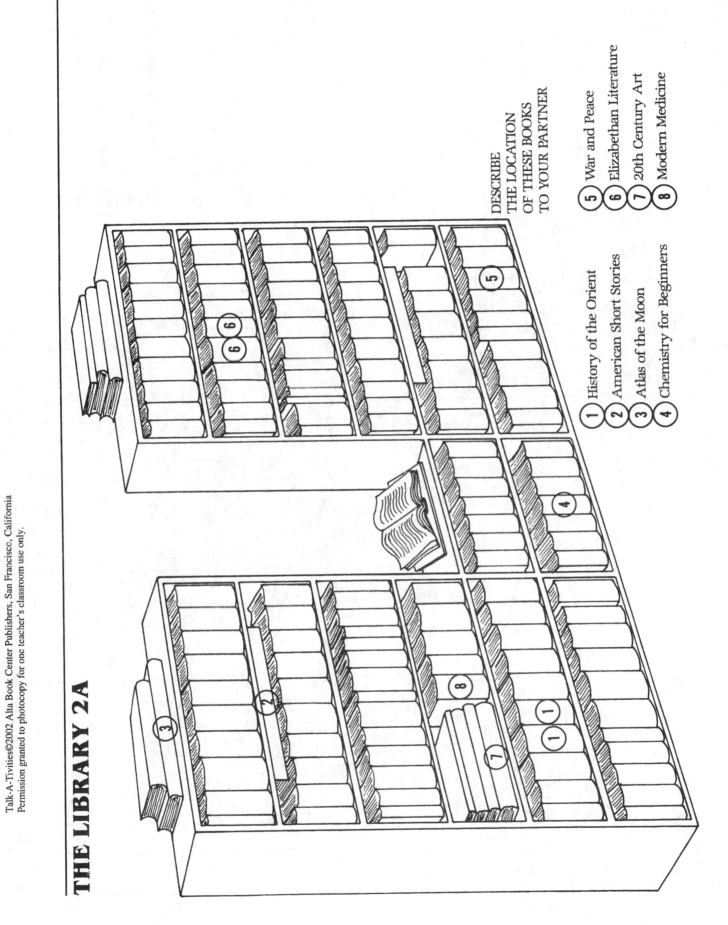

DESCRIBE
THE LOCATION
OF THESE BOOKS
TO YOUR PARTNER

1. History of the Orient
2. American Short Stories
3. Atlas of the Moon
4. Chemistry for Beginners
5. War and Peace
6. Elizabethan Literature
7. 20th Century Art
8. Modern Medicine

41

THE LIBRARY 2B

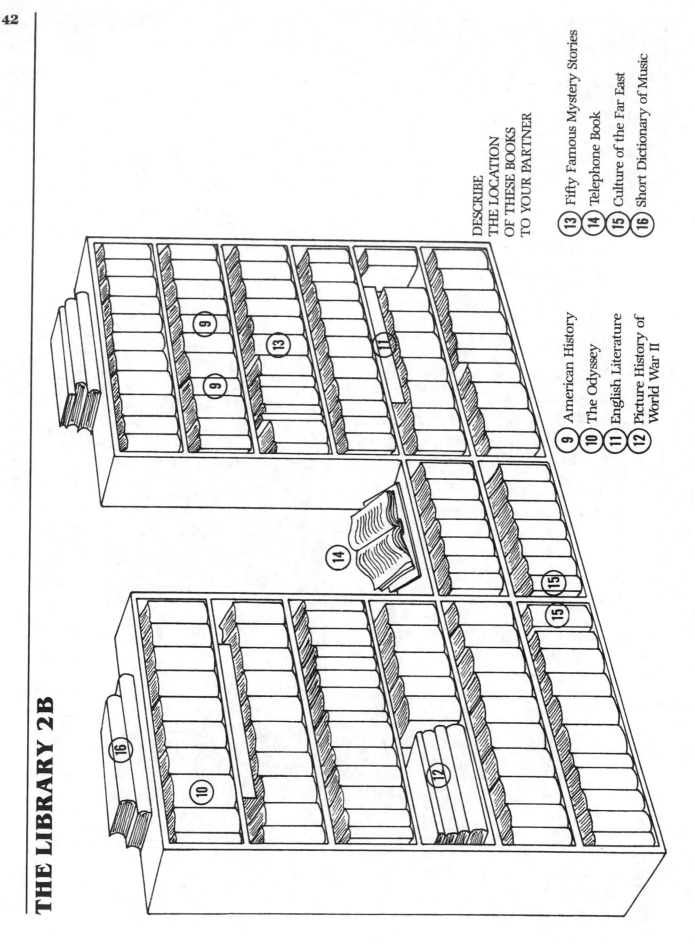

DESCRIBE
THE LOCATION
OF THESE BOOKS
TO YOUR PARTNER

9 American History
10 The Odyssey
11 English Literature
12 Picture History of World War II

13 Fifty Famous Mystery Stories
14 Telephone Book
15 Culture of the Far East
16 Short Dictionary of Music

There are two *ESL Supermarket* activities. It is probably best to use one or the other but not both with a particular student. Both activities use the same answer sheet.

Both activities provide practice in describing (and understanding descriptions of) locations. In addition, the second activity gives practice in classifying, a necessary subskill for outlining. Both activities will have immediate practical value in helping students better understand the way in which products are organized on the shelves of their local supermarkets.

Procedure (The ESL Supermarket 1)

a. Tell students that this activity is based on the plan of a small supermarket. They will be working in pairs and describing where certain foods can be found in the market.

b. Divide the class into pairs. Give one member of each pair the page labeled *The ESL Supermarket-1*. Give the other member the page labeled *The ESL Supermarket/Answers*. (If possible, give the *ESL Supermarket-1* page to the member of the pair who most needs practice in describing locations. Give the answer page to the member who most needs practice in understanding such descriptions. You may not be able to make such distinctions, however, since proficiency at one frequently means proficiency at the other.)

c. Call attention to the instructions on the two pages. Student B (with the answer sheet) is to ask Student A for the location of "the various foods you expect to be sold in a supermarket." Student B should think of as many foods as possible, but they should all be fairly common foods that most supermarkets would stock.

d. Student A, with the plan of the stocked supermarket at hand, must describe the location of each food requested by Student B. If the food requested is not on the plan, Student A can (depending on the instructions you give) either (1) tell Student B that the store does not sell that item or (2) write the item in an appropriate empty square and describe its location.

e. As Student A describes the location of a food, Student B writes the name of that food in the correct space on the answer sheet.

f. When Student B has requested locations of all the foods he or she can think of, the two students compare their papers to see how well communication and comprehension worked.

Procedure (The ESL Supermarket 2)

Follow steps *a* through *c* above, except that the sheet labeled *The ESL Supermarket-2* is used.

d. Student A has the task of arranging the food on the shelves of the supermarket. Using the list printed on the activity page, Student A writes the names of fifteen foods in appropriate squares, after having set up three "departments." Then, using the completed page, Student A describes the location of each food requested by Student B. As in step *d* above, you can instruct Student A either to tell Student B that a particular food is not sold by the store (if it has been omitted from Student A's diagram) or to insert it in an appropriate empty square.

Follow steps *e* and *f* above.

THE ESL SUPERMARKET-1

Directions: Study this plan of a supermarket. Be ready to describe the exact location of the things that your partner asks for.

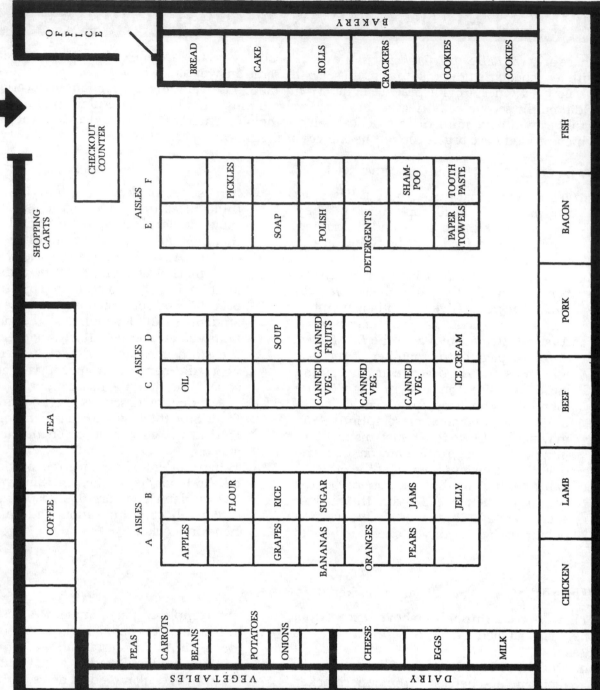

THE ESL SUPERMARKET-2

Directions. In each of the spaces marked X, write one of the following: FRUITS, VEGETABLES, MEATS, DAIRY, BAKERY. Then in any appropriate location, write *fifteen* of the following. Your partner will ask for their location.

apples
bananas
beans
beef
bread
cake
candy
carrots
cheese
chicken
coffee
fish
grapes
lamb
lettuce
milk
paper towels
pickles
pineapple
potatoes
soap
soup
tea
tomatoes

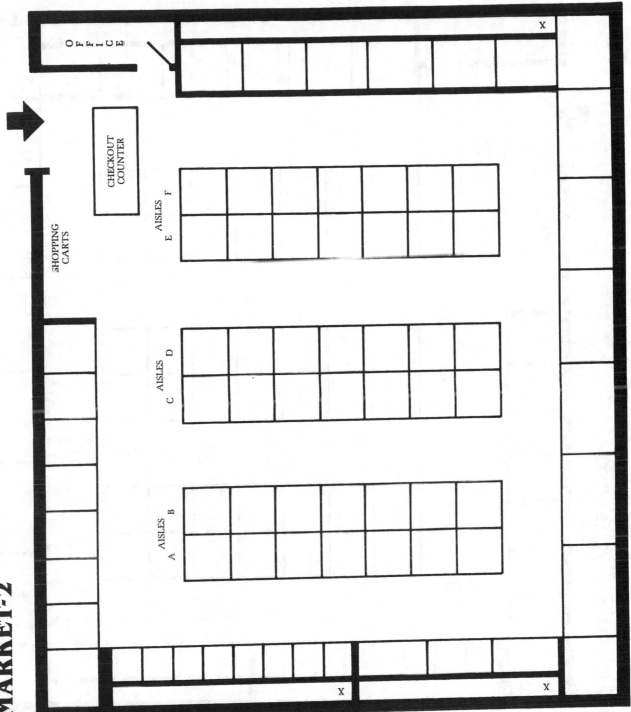

OFFICE

X

CHECKOUT COUNTER

SHOPPING CARTS

AISLES
A B

AISLES
C D

AISLES
E F

X

X

45

THE ESL SUPERMARKET / Answers

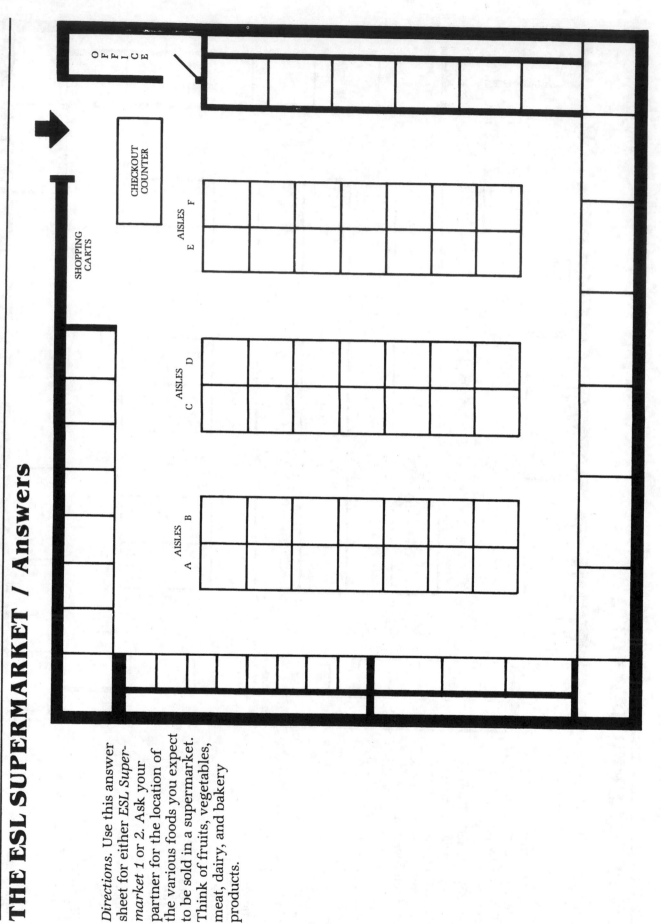

Directions. Use this answer sheet for either *ESL Supermarket 1 or 2.* Ask your partner for the location of the various foods you expect to be sold in a supermarket. Think of fruits, vegetables, meat, dairy, and bakery products.

CHECKOUT COUNTER

SHOPPING CARTS

OFFICE

AISLES A B

AISLES C D

AISLES E F

Talk-A-Tivities©2002 Alta Book Center Publishers, San Francisco, California
Permission granted to photocopy for one teacher's classroom use only.

This series of activities gives students some of the language that they will need to give and ask for directions. As an incidental dividend, it also provides practice in using maps to find one's way from one place to another.

Procedure

a. Use the practice page (Main Street and Central Avenue) for students who need review and practice in asking for and giving directions and locations. Review the sentence patterns in the center of the page, and be sure students are familiar with the compass directions (point out that if you are facing north, east is on your right, west on your left, and south behind you; review the names of the intercardinal points). In Practice A and B at the bottom of the page, have each student practice the patterns by asking for a location or directions; have another student answer.

b. Use any or all of the five map activities. These are sequenced roughly in order of difficulty. Students work in pairs for all five.

> *Center City 1 A* and *B:* Student A asks Student B how to get from the bus station to six locations which are identified on Student B's map but not on Student A's. As Student B gives the directions, Student A follows them, and then marks the location of the building on his/her map. When Student B has given (and Student A has followed) directions to all six locations, Student B then asks Student A how to get to six additional locations which are identified on Student A's map but not on Student B's. At the conclusion of the exercise, all twelve locations should be marked on both maps.

> *Center City 2 A* and *B:* Student A has Map A and an A&B Response Sheet. Student B has Map B and a Response Sheet. Student A describes the "errand route" on Map A to Student B, who records it on the Response Sheet. Student B then describes the errand route on Map B to Student A, who records it on his/her

response sheet. Students then compare their response sheets with Maps A and B for immediate feedback.

> *Midtown Manhattan A* and *B:* Using the keys on their maps, Students A and B describe locations in midtown Manhattan (New York City) to each other. Each marks these locations on his/her map, using the key letters or numbers to identify them. Students then compare maps.

> *Midtown Manhattan X* and *Y:* Students follow the same procedure as for Midtown Manhattan A and B.

> *London A* and *B:* Students ask each other to describe the locations of certain well-known places in London. Each student has the locations that will be requested circled and named on his/her map. The locations that the student will request are not, however, circled or named, so the student must locate them from the directions and information given by his/her partner. You may want to direct attention to the arrow showing north and elicit that students can determine the other compass points if they know where north is.

c. As students are working on these activities, circulate around the class to determine any difficulties students may be having. Provide help only if a pair seems to have come to an impasse.

d. When the activities have been completed, let students discuss how successful they were in communicating locations and directions to each other. Help them to pinpoint any specific problem areas, and discuss ways of handling these. You may want to follow up these activities with a map of your city or town and have students tell each other where they live and how to get there.

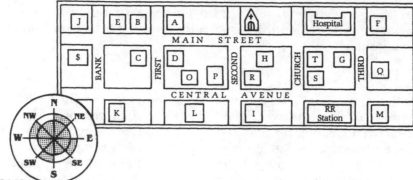

GIVING LOCATIONS

Main Street is north of Central Avenue.
Central is one block south of Main.

$$\left.\begin{array}{l} A \\ B \\ C \\ D \end{array}\right\} \text{is on the} \left[\begin{array}{l} \text{northeast} \\ \text{northwest} \\ \text{southwest} \\ \text{southeast} \end{array}\right] \text{corner of First and Main.}$$

A is diagonally across from C.

A is opposite D.
E is next to B.
H is between Second and Church, in the middle of the block, on the south side of Main.
G is three blocks east of C.

ASKING FOR DIRECTIONS

Excuse me, Pardon	can you (please) would you	tell me	where X is?		
			how	I can get to go	to X?

GIVING DIRECTIONS

From	here there the corner	go walk	one block north five blocks east across the park	and	turn left on Y Street. cross the street. go up X Street.

Go	out of X across the street to that corner	and	turn go walk	left/right north/east/ south/west	until you come to. . . two blocks. . .

PRACTICE

A. Describe the location of these places:

1. The railroad station	5. Building F	9. Building J
2. The hospital	6. Building G	10. Building K
3. The church	7. Building H	11. Building L
4. The bank	8. Building I	12. Building M

B. You are at the railroad station. Ask for directions to:

1. Building Q	3. Building E	5. Building K	7. The bank
2. Building P	4. The church	6. Building D	8. Building H

NOTE: Pay attention to the importance of *the*. For example:
I'm at J. Where is R? Go east on Main and turn right at the church.
I'm at J. Where is S? Go east on Main and turn right at Church.

Talk-A-Tivities©2002 Alta Book Center Publishers, San Francisco, California
Permission granted to photocopy for one teacher's classroom use only.

MAP ACTIVITY-1

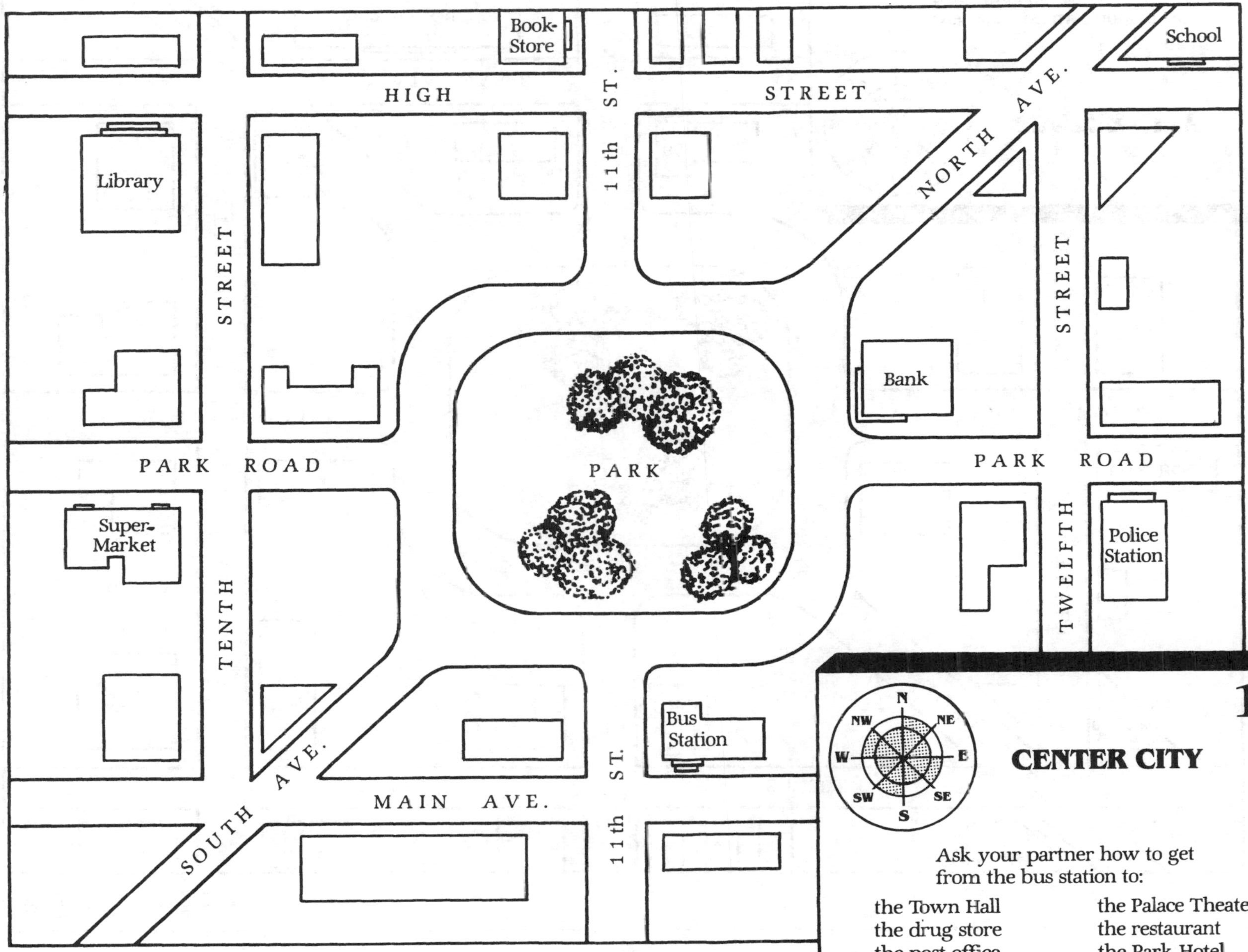

1A

CENTER CITY

Ask your partner how to get
from the bus station to:

the Town Hall   the Palace Theater
the drug store   the restaurant
the post office   the Park Hotel

School

PARK ROAD

Police
Station

TWELFTH   STREET

NORTH AVE.

Bank

STREET

HIGH

Book-
Store

11th ST.

PARK

Bus
Station

11th ST.

MAIN AVE.

SOUTH AVE.

PARK ROAD

TENTH   STREET

STREET

Library

Super-
Market

MAP ACTIVITY-1

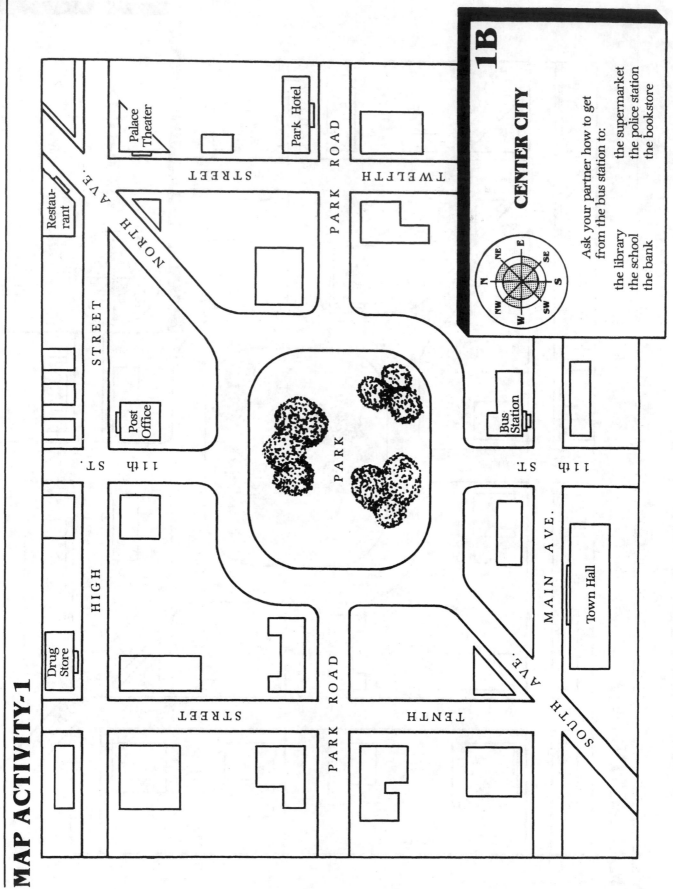

1B

CENTER CITY

Ask your partner how to get
from the bus station to:

the library   the supermarket
the school   the police station
the bank   the bookstore

MAP ACTIVITY-2

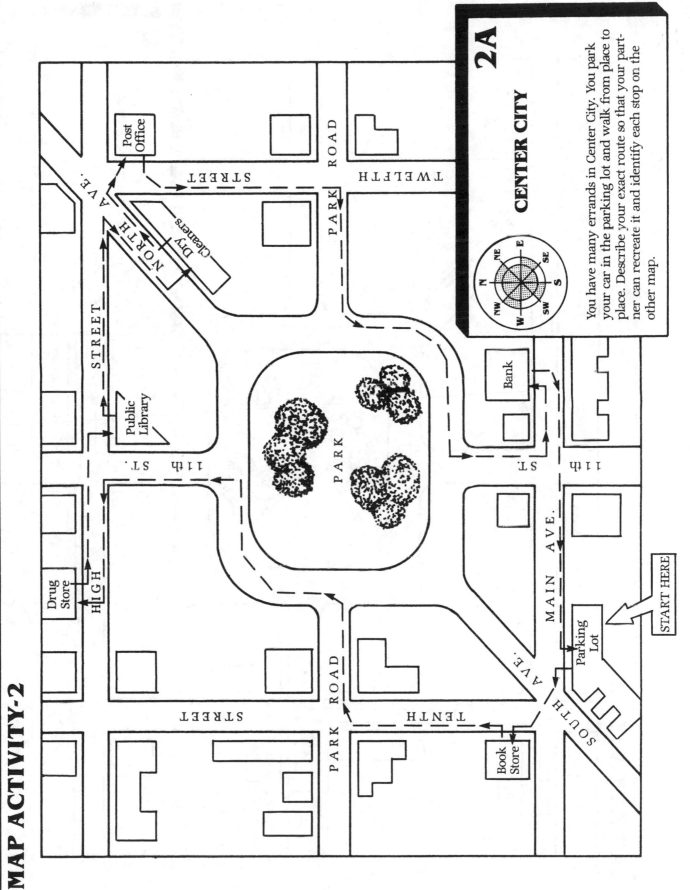

2A

CENTER CITY

You have many errands in Center City. You park your car in the parking lot and walk from place to place. Describe your exact route so that your partner can recreate it and identify each stop on the other map.

MAP ACTIVITY-2

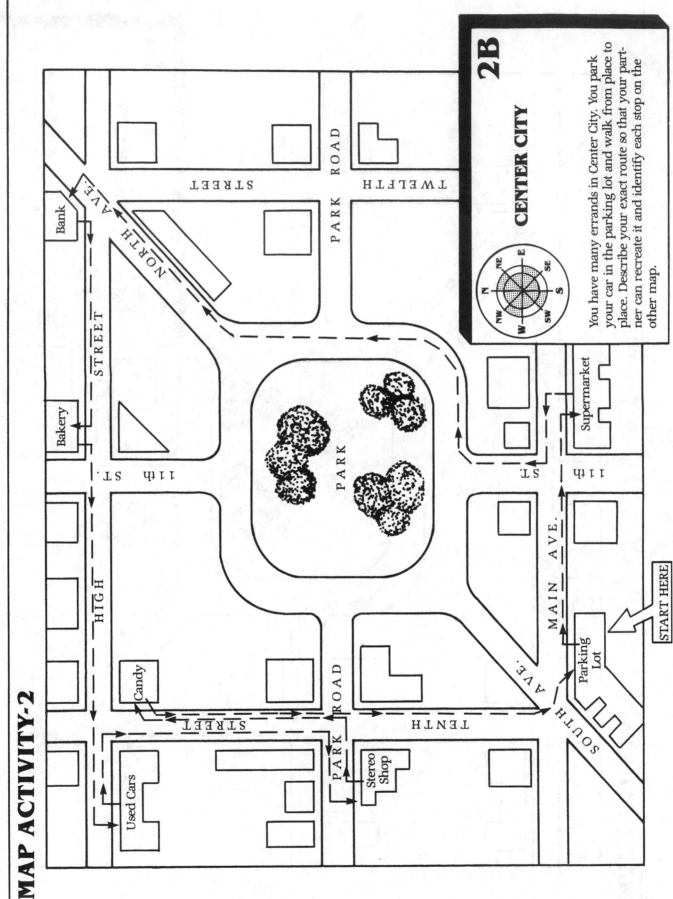

2B

CENTER CITY

You have many errands in Center City. You park your car in the parking lot and walk from place to place. Describe your exact route so that your partner can recreate it and identify each stop on the other map.

START HERE

MAP ACTIVITY-2

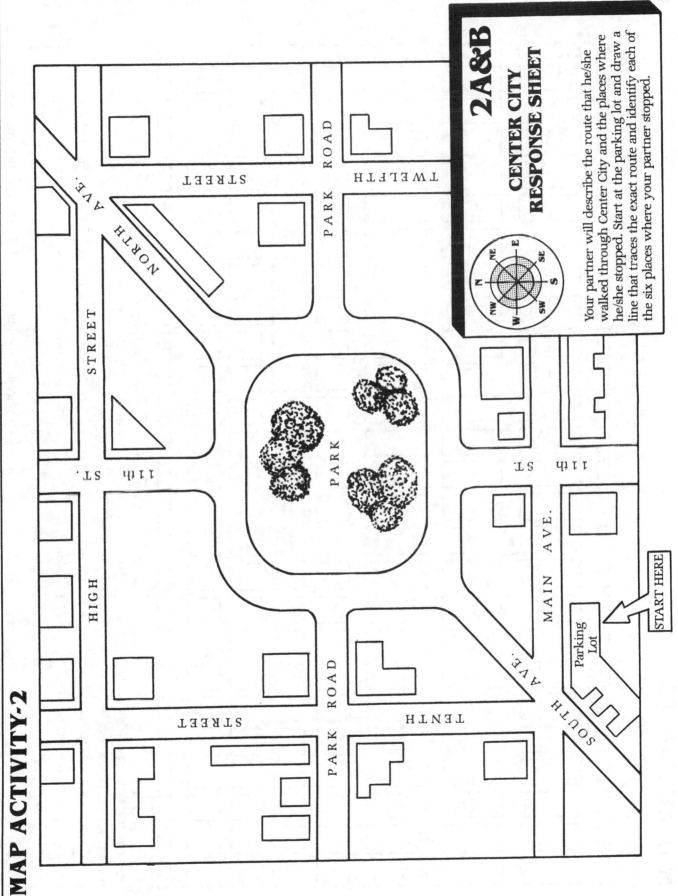

2A&B

CENTER CITY RESPONSE SHEET

Your partner will describe the route that he/she walked through Center City and the places where he/she stopped. Start at the parking lot and draw a line that traces the exact route and identify each of the six places where your partner stopped.

START HERE

Parking Lot

53

MAP ACTIVITY-3

57 St.
56 St.
55 St.
54 St.
53 St.
52 St.
51 St.
50 St.
49 St.
48 St.
47 St.
46 St.
45 St.
44 St.
43 St.
42 St.
41 St.
40 St.
39 St.
38 St.
37 St.
36 St.
35 St.
34 St.
33 St.

EIGHTH AVENUE
SEVENTH AVENUE
BROADWAY
SIXTH AVENUE
FIFTH AVENUE
MADISON AVENUE
PARK AVENUE
LEXINGTON AVENUE
THIRD AVENUE

Ⓐ Ⓑ Ⓒ Ⓓ Ⓔ Ⓕ Ⓖ Ⓗ

N E W S

Study the locations of the following places. Be ready to describe the exact location of each place that your partner asks about.

Ask your partner for, and mark the exact location of, each of the following places in midtown Manhattan:

MAP A MIDTOWN MANHATTAN

Ⓐ St. Patrick's Cathedral
Ⓑ Macy's Department Store
Ⓒ Cartier's Jewelry
Ⓓ Times Square
Ⓔ Belasco Theater
Ⓕ Time-Life Building
Ⓖ Grand Central Station
Ⓗ Exxon Building

① New York Hilton Hotel
② Herald Square
③ Radio City Music Hall
④ Chrysler Building
⑤ McGraw-Hill Book Co.
⑥ Empire State Building
⑦ Museum of Modern Art
⑧ Gimbel's Department Store

MAP ACTIVITY-3

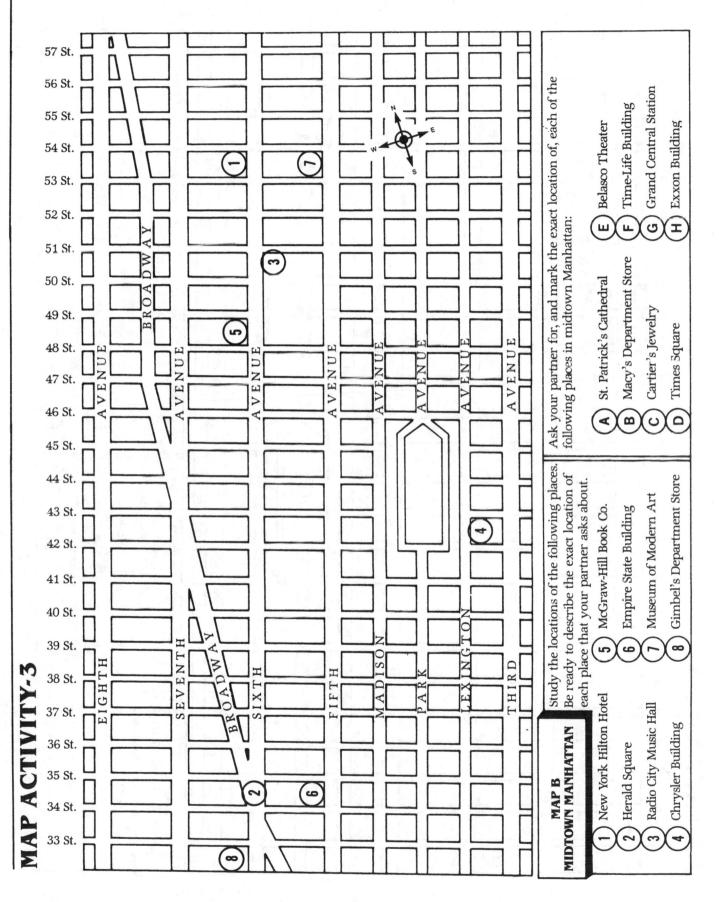

**MAP B
MIDTOWN MANHATTAN**

Study the locations of the following places.
Be ready to describe the exact location of
each place that your partner asks about.

1. New York Hilton Hotel
2. Herald Square
3. Radio City Music Hall
4. Chrysler Building
5. McGraw-Hill Book Co.
6. Empire State Building
7. Museum of Modern Art
8. Gimbel's Department Store

Ask your partner for, and mark the exact location of, each of the
following places in midtown Manhattan:

A. St. Patrick's Cathedral
B. Macy's Department Store
C. Cartier's Jewelry
D. Times Square
E. Belasco Theater
F. Time-Life Building
G. Grand Central Station
H. Exxon Building

MAP ACTIVITY-4

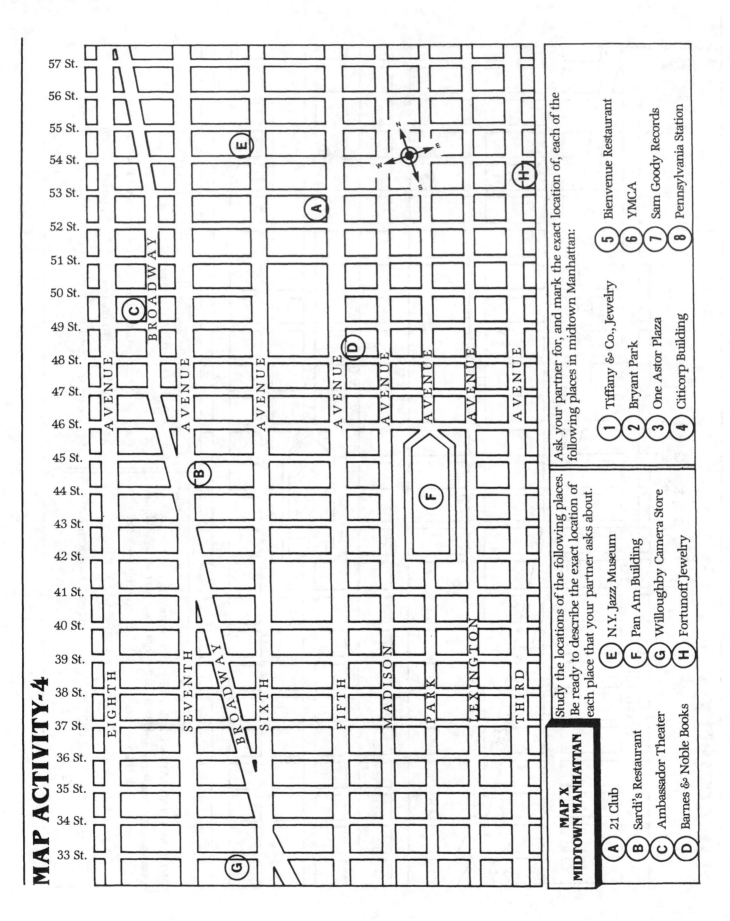

MAP X
MIDTOWN MANHATTAN

Study the locations of the following places. Be ready to describe the exact location of each place that your partner asks about.

- Ⓐ 21 Club
- Ⓑ Sardi's Restaurant
- Ⓒ Ambassador Theater
- Ⓓ Barnes & Noble Books
- Ⓔ N.Y. Jazz Museum
- Ⓕ Pan Am Building
- Ⓖ Willoughby Camera Store
- Ⓗ Fortunoff Jewelry

Ask your partner for, and mark the exact location of, each of the following places in midtown Manhattan:

- ① Tiffany & Co., Jewelry
- ② Bryant Park
- ③ One Astor Plaza
- ④ Citicorp Building
- ⑤ Bienvenue Restaurant
- ⑥ YMCA
- ⑦ Sam Goody Records
- ⑧ Pennsylvania Station

MAP ACTIVITY-4

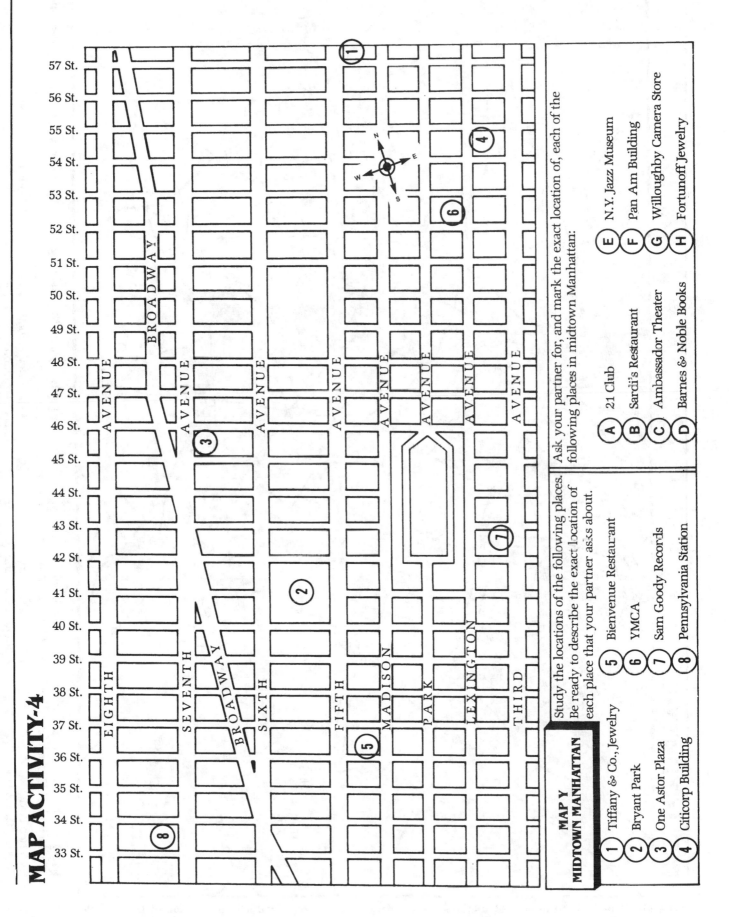

MAP Y MIDTOWN MANHATTAN

Study the locations of the following places. Be ready to describe the exact location of each place that your partner asks about.

1. Tiffany & Co., Jewelry
2. Bryant Park
3. One Astor Plaza
4. Citicorp Building
5. Bienvenue Restaurant
6. YMCA
7. Sam Goody Records
8. Pennsylvania Station

Ask your partner for, and mark the exact location of, each of the following places in midtown Manhattan:

A. 21 Club
B. Sardi's Restaurant
C. Ambassador Theater
D. Barnes & Noble Books
E. N.Y. Jazz Museum
F. Pan Am Building
G. Willoughby Camera Store
H. Fortunoff Jewelry

58

MAP ACTIVITY-5

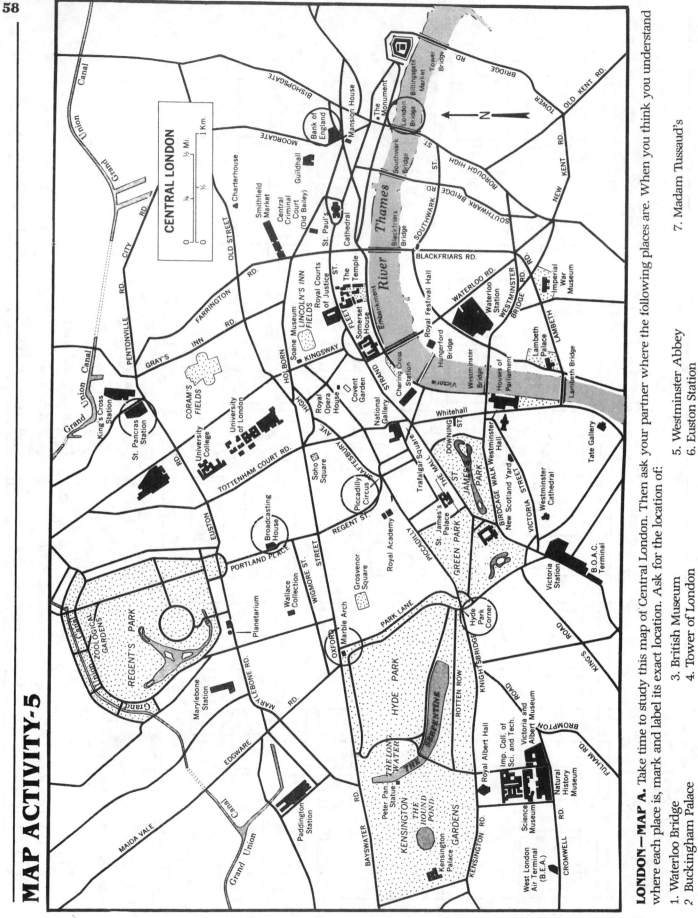

CENTRAL LONDON

0   ¼   ½ Mi.

0   ½   1 Km.

LONDON—MAP A. Take time to study this map of Central London. Then ask your partner where the following places are. When you think you understand where each place is, mark and label its exact location. Ask for the location of:

1. Waterloo Bridge
2. Buckingham Palace
3. British Museum
4. Tower of London
5. Westminster Abbey
6. Euston Station
7. Madam Tussaud's

MAP ACTIVITY-5

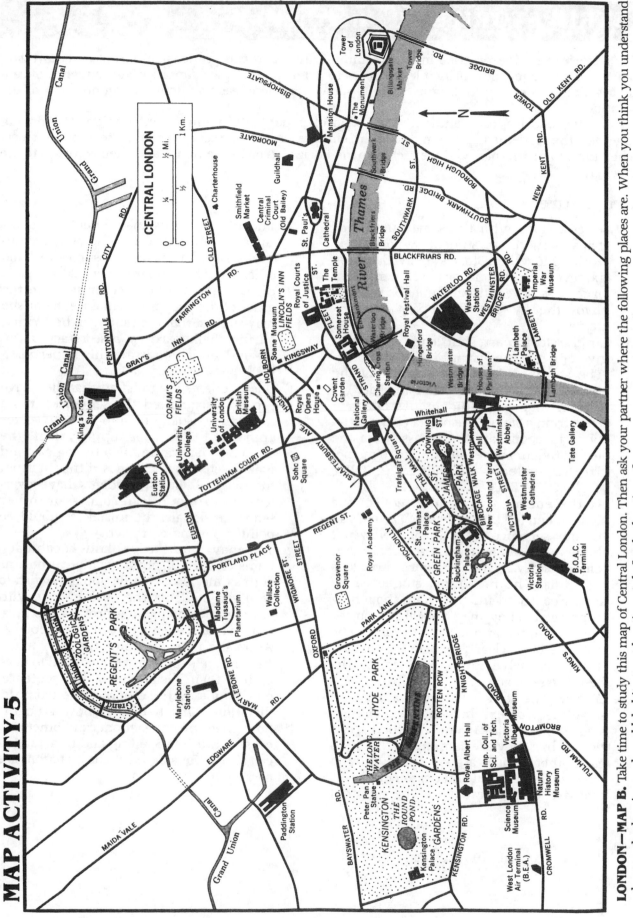

LONDON—MAP B. Take time to study this map of Central London. Then ask your partner where the following places are. When you think you understand where each place is, mark and label its exact location. Ask for the location of:

1. London Bridge
2. Piccadilly Circus

3. Bank of England
4. Hyde Park Corner

5. St. Pancras Station
6. Broadcasting House

7. Marble Arch

Strip Stories provide practice in oral communication and comprehension and also require students to apply rhetorical principles in order to determine a logical, appropriate sequence of sentences. Students cooperate linguistically to solve a problem, each student having one part of the solution.

In Strip Stories, each student has a strip of paper with a single sentence on it. Working together, the students must combine their sentences in the correct order to make a logical story. They have to do this orally, since each is to memorize his or her sentence and then return it to the teacher.

Procedure

a. Select a story with the same number of strips as there are students who will be working together. Stories are available for six, seven, eight, nine, or ten students. In a large class, several stories may be worked on together by several groups of appropriate size.

b. Cut the story apart, shuffle the strips, and give one sentence (strip) to each student. (The shuffling is to make sure that the strips are distributed in random order.)

c. Explain that each student has one sentence from a story. The object of the activity is to cooperate and reassemble the story. Students have one minute to memorize the sentence on their strip. THEY MAY NOT WRITE ANYTHING.

d. At the end of the minute, collect the strips. Then tell the students, "Each of you has one sentence from a story. Now put the sentences together in correct order to tell the story." Give no more directions than this. The first time, students may appear confused and uncertain about how to proceed. They may appeal to you for further information. Say nothing. The task has been clearly explained; the students themselves must now decide the best course of action.

e. Observe the students as they attempt to solve the problem, but under no circumstances make any comments or corrections while they are communicating with each other. This is a good opportunity to observe the cultural and personality traits that are demonstrated by the different students. Students may interrupt, overlap, and contradict each other, but eventually one student usually assumes the role of leader. This student may ask others to repeat sentences or to sit or stand in the order of the proposed sequence; he or she may suggest that the sentences be written on the chalkboard by a secretary or by the individual students; this is permissible.

f. Once students are satisfied that they have properly sequenced the sentences into a story, they usually turn to the teacher for approval. Give this approval if the sequence is grammatically logical and makes sense, even if it is different from the original. But if students have overlooked pronoun references or other sequence signals, the mistakes should be pointed out and corrected.

g. You may want to explain vocabulary items or correct pronunciation problems at this time, also. Finally, you may wish to read the students the entire story with clear enunciation and appropriate expression so that students hear it as a whole.

h. As an alternate to reading the story to the students, it is sometimes beneficial to have each of them dictate his or her sentence, one by one, as the others write from the dictation. This helps to show students how their pronunciation can sometimes cause confusion. Spelling and punctuation can also be considered as the dictations are corrected.

STRIP STORY FOR
SIX STUDENTS (The Fortune Teller)

I don't like to make major decisions without first consulting a fortune teller.

I went to Madame LaZonga, who demanded ten dollars.

Furthermore, she told me, I was allowed to ask her only two questions.

I protested that this was unfair and more expensive than usual.

"Isn't ten dollars a lot of money for just two questions?" I asked.

"Yes," she answered. "Second question, please."

STRIP STORY FOR
SIX STUDENTS (The Big Boys)

One bright morning in the middle of the night,	Two big boys got up to fight.
Back to back, they faced each other,	Drew their swords and shot each other.
A deaf policeman heard the noise.	He came and arrested those two big boys.

STRIP STORY FOR
SEVEN STUDENTS (The Tea Bag)

Americans are quite used to the convenience of packaged products.

Some foreigners, however, are sometimes confused by them.

One day I was having tea at the Palace Cafeteria with a student from another country.

He tore open the little tea bag and emptied the tea into his cup.

I explained that the bag itself was meant to be dipped, unopened, into the water.

He was surprised and thanked me for correcting him.

Then he confidently put an unopened envelope of sugar into his cup of tea.

STRIP STORY FOR
SEVEN STUDENTS (Montreal for Christmas)

Mr. and Mrs. Jones are Canadians who now live in Miami.

They often drive back to Canada for holidays.

One year they decided to drive up to Montreal for Christmas.

It was snowing hard when they reached the US-Canada border.

The customs official looked at their Florida license plates.

"You can go through without a customs inspection," he said.

"Anyone dumb enough to leave Florida at this time of year can't be smart enough to smuggle anything."

STRIP STORY FOR
EIGHT STUDENTS (The Theater)

Last week I went to the theater.

I had a very good seat and the play was interesting.

But I could not enjoy it because a young man and woman were sitting behind me.

They were talking very loudly.

Because I could not hear the actors on stage, I became very angry.

I turned around and told them, "I can't hear a word!"

"It's none of your business," the young man said.

"This is a private conversation."

STRIP STORY FOR
EIGHT STUDENTS (Jack's Career)

Jack started work as a janitor in the XYZ Company.	Within six months he became a salesman.
Only a year later he became vice-president of the company.	A few days later the president called Jack into his office.
The president explained that he would retire soon and Jack would become president.	Jack said, "Thanks."
The president said, "You have been here less than two years and all you can say is thanks?"	"Well," Jack replied, "Thanks a lot, Dad."

STRIP STORY FOR
EIGHT STUDENTS (Cafeteria Food)

Talk-A-Tivities©2002 Alta Book Center Publishers, San Francisco, California
Permission granted to photocopy for one teacher's classroom use only.

One day the school dean ate lunch in the cafeteria.	He wanted to know how the students liked the food.
He asked a group of students, "How do you like the food here?"	One student answered, "We fight over it all the time."
The dean was pleased to hear this.	He exclaimed, "So it's that good, is it?"
"Not exactly, sir," the student replied.	"The loser has to eat it."

STRIP STORY FOR
NINE STUDENTS (The Student Who Overslept)

My friend usually gets up at 7:00.	But this morning he slept until 7:30.
When he realized he had overslept, he leaped out of bed.	First he showered and shaved.
Then he got dressed.	At 8:00 he ate his breakfast quickly.
He rushed out of the house to catch the 8:15 bus.	He arrived at school just in time for class.
By 9:00 he was sound asleep again, this time with his head on the desk.	

Talk-A-Tivities©2002 Alta Book Center Publishers, San Francisco, California
Permission granted to photocopy for one teacher's classroom use only.

STRIP STORY FOR
TEN STUDENTS (The Two Men Fishing)

One day two men went fishing.

They rented a rowboat and rowed into the middle of the lake.

They were lucky and caught a lot of fish.

They caught so many that they wanted to be sure of the exact place.

Then they could return the next day and catch many more fish.

"How can we remember this exact place?" one of the men asked the other.

"That's easy," the other man replied.

"I'll paint an X on the side of the boat right over this place in the lake."

"But that's stupid!" the first man said.

"How can we be sure that we'll get the same boat?"

Crossword Partners is the first of three kinds of crossword puzzles that require communicative action between two students. Each partner has only one part of the puzzle and depends upon information from the other in order to solve it. The effectiveness of the students' communication is immediately confirmed when the two partners look at the completed puzzle. Because two of these kinds of puzzles require students to make up their own definitions, you may want to spend a few minutes reviewing how to define words, using explanations such as the following.

nouns: to define a noun (*kitchen,* for example), start with a general statement: *a kitchen is a room.* Then add a phrase or clause that differentiates the item from others of the same general kind; in this case you might add, *that is used for cooking.* The final definition (after the original noun has been dropped) is *a room used for cooking.* Let students practice defining these nouns: *dictionary, bed, nurse, submarine, elephant, price, snow, thunder.*

verbs: to define a verb, use a synonym (*exit means to leave or go out of a room*) or describe the action (*kneel means to get down on your knees*) or explain who does the action when and where (*sleep is something we all do, usu-ally in bed, with our eyes closed, and many of us wear pajamas or nightgowns while doing it*). Let students practice defining *repeat, shut, dance, instruct, request, ski.*

adjectives: to define an adjective use a synonym (*beautiful means pretty or attractive*), or antonym (*sad is the opposite of happy* or *sad means not happy*).

Tell students to try to avoid using another form of the word in their definitions. Instead of defining *driver* as *a person who drives a car,* students should use something like *a person who steers a car* or *a person who operates an automobile.*

Procedure

a. Divide the class into pairs. Give Student A a copy of the *Across Partner* page. Give Student B a copy of the *Down Partner* page.

b. Tell the students that they are to work together to complete the puzzles. They must not look at each other's puzzle.

Each is to ask the other for definitions of the other's words and provide definitions for the words asked for.

c. When both students have filled in their words, they compare puzzles to check the correct answers.

Answer keys may be made by combining the Across and Down pages for each puzzle . The five puzzles are in approximate order of difficulty.

Complete this puzzle by cooperating with your partner. Ask each other for *definitions* of the missing words. For example:

"What's 20 across?"
"It's a four-legged animal that cowboys ride."

Do not use a form of the word in your definition of the word. For example: (A teacher) It's someone who teaches.

Complete this puzzle by cooperating with your partner. Ask each other for *definitions* of the missing words. For example:

"What's 20 across?"
"It's a four-legged animal that cowboys ride."

Do not use a form of the word in your definition of the word. For example: (A teacher) It's someone who teaches.

Complete this puzzle by cooperating with your partner. Ask each other for *definitions* of the missing words. For example:

"What's 20 across?"
"It's a four-legged animal that cowboys ride."

Do not use a form of the word in your definition of the word. For example: (A teacher) It's someone who teaches.

Complete this puzzle by cooperating with your partner. Ask each other for *definitions* of the missing words. For example:

"What's 20 across?"
"It's a four-legged animal that cowboys ride."

Do not use a form of the word in your definition of the word. For example: (A teacher) It's someone who teaches.

Complete this puzzle by cooperating with your partner. Ask each other for *definitions* of the missing words. For example:

"What's 20 across?"
"It's a four-legged animal that cowboys ride."

Do not use a form of the word in your definition of the word. For example: (A teacher) It's someone who teaches.

Complete this puzzle by cooperating with your partner. Ask each other for *definitions* of the missing words. For example:

"What's 20 across?"
"It's a four-legged animal that cowboys ride."

Do not use a form of the word in your definition of the word. For example: (A teacher) It's someone who teaches.

Talk-A-Tivities©2002 Alta Book Center Publishers, San Francisco, California
Permission granted to photocopy for one teacher's classroom use only.

All the words in this puzzle refer to professions, occupations, or things that people do for fun or profit. To complete your puzzle, cooperate with your partner. Ask each other for *definitions* of the missing words. For example: "What's 20 across?" "It's a person who cuts and sells meat." Do not use a form of the word in your definition of the word!

Talk-A-Tivities©2002 Alta Book Center Publishers, San Francisco, California
Permission granted to photocopy for one teacher's classroom use only.

CROSSWORD PARTNERS-4

All the words in this puzzle refer to professions, occupations, or things that people do for fun or profit. To complete your puzzle, cooperate with your partner. Ask each other for *definitions* of the missing words. For example: "What's 20 across?" "It's a person who cuts and sells meat." Do not use a form of the word in your definition of the word!

Talk-A-Tivities©2002 Alta Book Center Publishers, San Francisco, California
Permission granted to photocopy for one teacher's classroom use only.

Complete this puzzle by cooperating with your partner. Ask each other for *definitions* of the missing words. For example:

"What's 20 across?"
"It's a four-legged animal that cowboys ride."

Do not use a form of the word in your definition of the word. For example: (A teacher) It's someone who teaches.

Complete this puzzle by cooperating with your partner. Ask each other for *definitions* of the missing words. For example:

"What's 20 across?"
"It's a four-legged animal that cowboys ride."

Do not use a form of the word in your definition of the word. For example: (A teacher) It's someone who teaches.

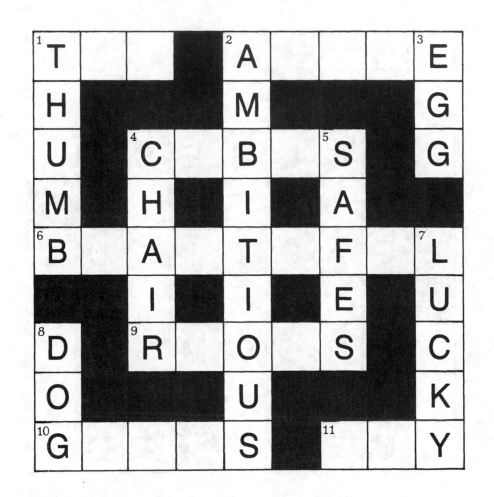

Talk-A-Tivities©2002 Alta Book Center Publishers, San Francisco, California
Permission granted to photocopy for one teacher's classroom use only.

COOPERATIVE CROSSWORD PUZZLES
Instructions & Answers

For these puzzles, one partner has the puzzle diagram and the other has the definitions. They cannot look at each other's pages and so must cooperate to solve the puzzle verbally, not visually.

Procedure

a. Divide the class into pairs. Give Student A in each pair the puzzle diagram and Student B the definitions. The five puzzles are in approximate order of difficulty, and you may want to have some students working on the earlier puzzles and others on the later ones—or have all pairs doing the same puzzle, and then going on to more difficult ones.

b. Describe the puzzle to the students and emphasize that members of a pair must not look at each other's papers. Read (or have students read) the instructions at the top of the A page and those at the top of the B page. (These instructions are the same for all five puzzles.) Be sure students understand what they are to do. Point out that the definitions include sentences in which the word is used. Tell students that when they read these sentences to their partners, they are to use the word "blank" when they come to the blank in the sentence. If all pairs are using the same puzzle, you may want to read the first definition aloud to demonstrate how Student B should read it to Student A.

c. Tell the students that they are to work together to get the answers. Student A may tell Student B how many letters the answer includes, and as the puzzle is filled in, what letters are already in place. Either student can suggest possible words, but only Student A can write them in the puzzle.

f. When the puzzles are completed, Students A and B can show each other their pages. If all pairs have been working on the same puzzle, different students can volunteer answers for the different definitions and can make up additional sentences that use the words.

Answer Key

Puzzle 1: *Across:* (1) address, (5) is, (6) learn, (8) river, (9) go, (10) explore.
        Down: (2) describe, (3) even, (4) stranger, (7) keep.

Puzzle 2: *Across:* (1) speaker, (5) he, (6) world, (8) lunch, (9) it, (10) evening.
        Down: (2) pressure, (3) know, (4) religion, (7) ache.

Puzzle 3: *Across:* (1) gun, (3) met, (5) satisfy, (6) private, (8) pig, (9) eye.
        Down: (1) gas, (2) nothing, (3) mistake, (4) toy, (6) pop, (7) eve.

Puzzle 4: *Across:* (1) politics, (4) lies, (6) end, (7) paw, (8) sand, (10) examples.
        Down: (1) postpone, (2) toe, (3) soldiers, (4) laws, (5) send, (9) arm.

Puzzle 5: *Across:* (2) left, (5) eat, (7) pot, (9) middle, (10) too, (11) ask, (12) rulers, (14) our, (15) on, (16) raw, (17) tea, (19) few.
        Down: (1) wet, (3) food, (4) go, (6) tomorrow, (7) pleasant, (8) ticket, (10) toward, (13) large, (18) at.

COOPERATIVE CROSSWORD PUZZLE-1A

In order to solve this crossword puzzle, you will have to cooperate with a partner. You have the puzzle; your partner has the definitions. Ask your partner for each of the definitions. For example, "What's the definition of the word for 2 across?" or "What is 2 down?" You may ask your partner for any help you want, but you may not look at the definitions and your partner may not look at the puzzle. In other words, you can cooperate verbally but not visually!

Talk-A-Tivities©2002 Alta Book Center Publishers, San Francisco, California
Permission granted to photocopy for one teacher's classroom use only.

COOPERATIVE CROSSWORD PUZZLE-1B

In order to solve this crossword puzzle, you will have to cooperate with your partner. You have only the definitions and example sentences; your partner has the puzzle. Read, and if necessary, explain the definition when your partner asks. You may not look at the puzzle and your partner may not look at the definitions. In other words, you may cooperate verbally but not visually!

ACROSS

1. The number of the building, the name of the street, town and country where you live. *When you write me, be sure to write my name and _____ clearly on the envelope.*

5. Present tense, third person singular, *be*. *What _____ the correct grammatical form?*

6. To gain knowledge or skill. *Be sure to _____ all the irregular verb forms in English.*

8. A wide natural stream of flowing water. *People live on both sides of the _____ just before it flows into the lake.*

9. To leave the place where you are. *Because I couldn't _____ home for the holiday, I asked my family to come to visit me.*

10. To travel to a place for the purpose of discovery. *Samuel de Champlain sailed from France in order to _____ the Quebec area of what is now Canada.*

DOWN

2. To give a picture of something or someone in words. *The teacher asked me to _____ the capital of my country.*

3. (Of numbers) that which can be divided by two with no remainder. *2, 4, 6, 8, are _____ numbers.*

4. A person who is unfamiliar. *When the woman returned to her hometown after so many years, no one recognized her and everyone treated her as a _____.*

7. To have something without the need to return it. *Here's more money than you need; you can _____ the change.*

COOPERATIVE CROSSWORD PUZZLE-2A

In order to solve this crossword puzzle, you will have to cooperate with a partner. You have the puzzle; your partner has the definitions. Ask your partner for each of the definitions. For example, "What's the definition of the word for 2 across?" or "What is 2 down?" You may ask your partner for any help you want, but you may not look at the definitions and your partner may not look at the puzzle. In other words, you can cooperate verbally but not visually!

COOPERATIVE CROSSWORD PUZZLE-2B

In order to solve this crossword puzzle, you will have to cooperate with your partner. You have only the definitions and example sentences; your partner has the puzzle. Read, and if necessary, explain the definition when your partner asks. You may not look at the puzzle and your partner may not look at the definitions. In other words, you may cooperate verbally but not visually!

ACROSS

1. A person making a speech. *There was a very interesting _____ at the conference.*

5. Third person singular subject pronoun. *My brother speaks good English, but _____ doesn't speak it as well as I do.*

6. The earth. *There are over 150 countries in the _____ today.*

8. The noon meal. *When I eat a lot for breakfast, I don't like to have much for _____.*

9. Third person singular pronoun, subject or object. *Mary heard a noise but didn't know what caused _____.*

10. The early part of the night, between the end of the day's work and bedtime. *After dinner, we spent the _____ talking about our holiday.*

DOWN

2. The force of the weight of the air. *Low atmospheric _____ means that it will rain.*

3. To have learned something. *I _____ how to speak some Arabic, but I don't _____ how to write it.*

4. A belief in one or more gods. *The couple were happily married, even though they each had a different _____.*

7. A continuous pain. *Such loud music makes my head _____.*

COOPERATIVE CROSSWORD PUZZLE-3A

In order to solve this crossword puzzle, you will have to cooperate with a partner. You have the puzzle; your partner has the definitions. Ask your partner for each of the definitions. For example, "What's the definition of the word for 2 across?" or "What is 2 down?" You may ask your partner for any help you want, but you may not look at the definitions and your partner may not look at the puzzle. In other words, you can cooperate verbally but not visually!

COOPERATIVE CROSSWORD PUZZLE-3B

In order to solve this crossword puzzle, you will have to cooperate with your partner. You have only the definitions and example sentences; your partner has the puzzle. Read, and if necessary, explain the definition when your partner asks. You may not look at the puzzle and your partner may not look at the definitions. In other words, you may cooperate verbally but not visually!

ACROSS

1. A weapon which shoots bullets. *The hunter quickly raised the _____ and pulled the trigger.*

3. To come together with someone by chance or arrangement (past tense). *Last night she _____ an old school friend on the street.*

5. To give enough; to fulfill a need or desire. *The book about birds was interesting but didn't _____ my curiosity to know more about birdsongs.*

6. Personal; not shared with others. *Paul's diary is _____; he will never show it to anyone else.*

8. A farm animal from which we get bacon and ham. *Because many people think a _____ is a dirty animal, they may tell a messy person, "Don't be such a _____!"*

9. The organ of sight; human beings have two. *After the accident, he lost his sight in one _____.*

DOWN

1. A petroleum product, used as a fuel in automobiles. *The price of _____ is so expensive now that people are driving less.*

2. Not any thing. *This box is empty; there's _____ in it.*

3. An error. *You made a serious _____ in addition; 21 + 13 is 34, not 36.*

4. Something a child plays with. *A doll is often a small child's favorite _____.*

6. A short, explosive sound, such as a cork makes when removed from a bottle. *A spark shot from the fireplace with a loud _____.*

7. The night before a religious feast or a holiday. *What did you do on New Year's _____?*

COOPERATIVE CROSSWORD PUZZLE-4A

In order to solve this crossword puzzle, you will have to cooperate with a partner. You have the puzzle; your partner has the definitions. Ask your partner for each of the definitions. For example, "What's the definition of the word for 2 across?" or "What is 2 down?" You may ask your partner for any help you want, but you may not look at the definitions and your partner may not look at the puzzle. In other words, you can cooperate verbally but not visually!

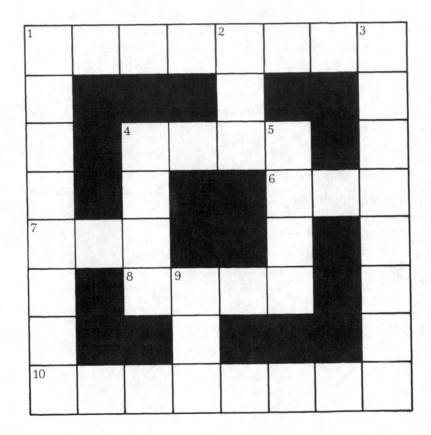

Talk-A-Tivities©2002 Alta Book Center Publishers, San Francisco, California
Permission granted to photocopy for one teacher's classroom use only.

COOPERATIVE CROSSWORD PUZZLE-4B

In order to solve this crossword puzzle, you will have to cooperate with your partner. You have only the definitions and example sentences; your partner has the puzzle. Read, and if necessary, explain the definition when your partner asks. You may not look at the puzzle and your partner may not look at the definitions. In other words, you may cooperate verbally but not visually!

ACROSS

1. The art or science of government. *John went into _____ and ran for a seat on the town council.*

4. Untrue statements. *The child told so many _____ that no one ever believed her.*

6. The point where something stops. *I'm very tired by the _____ of the day.*

7. An animal's foot. *The cat held the mouse under its _____.*

8. Very fine grains of loose material, found on beaches. *Children enjoy building castles in the _____ when they're at the seashore.*

10. Models that demonstrate a quality or a way of doing something. *The teacher showed her class some _____ of good writing.*

DOWN

1. To delay; to schedule for a later time. *Because of the rain, we had to _____ our picnic.*

2. One of the five small movable parts at the end of a foot. *Jack broke a _____ when he dropped a hammer on his foot.*

3. Members of an army. *During the battle, many _____ were wounded.*

4. Rules that are passed and supported by government to control the behavior of its citizens. *People are expected to obey the _____ of their country.*

5. To cause something to go or be taken to a place. *When you're in Hawaii, be sure to _____ me a postcard.*

9. One of the two upper limbs of a human being. *The sailor had a tattoo on his left _____, just above his elbow.*

COOPERATIVE CROSSWORD PUZZLE-5A

In order to solve this crossword puzzle, you will have to cooperate with your partner. You have the puzzle; your partner has the definitions. Ask your partner for each of the definitions. For example, "What's the definition of the word for 2 across?" or "What is 2 down?" You may ask your partner for any help you want, but you may not look at the definitions and your partner may not look at the puzzle. In other words, you can cooperate verbally but not visually!

COOPERATIVE CROSSWORD PUZZLE-5B

In order to solve this crossword puzzle, you will have to cooperate with your partner. You have only the definitions and example sentences; your partner has the puzzle. Read, and if necessary, explain the definition when your partner asks. You may not look at the puzzle and your partner may not look at the definitions. In other words, you may cooperate verbally but not visually!

ACROSS

2. Opposite of right. *Do you write with your right or _____ hand?*

5. To put food in your mouth, chew, and swallow it. *You should _____ a good breakfast every morning.*

7. A container used in cooking. *There's a nice hot _____ of soup on the stove.*

9. The central point. *She planted roses in the _____ of her garden.*

10. More than enough. *Maria ate _____ much ice cream and became sick.*

11. To request an answer from someone; to inquire. *I don't know why the sky is blue. Why don't you _____ your teacher?*

12. A long narrow flat object, used for drawing straight lines (plural). *The bookstore gave free _____ to all the students.*

14. Possessive pronoun: belonging to us. *_____ English teacher helps us a lot.*

15. Preposition: touching a surface. *Paul put his comic book _____ the teacher's desk.*

16. Not cooked. *Some people like to eat _____ vegetables.*

17. A hot brown drink made by pouring boiling water over dried leaves. *Some people drink _____ in the afternoon, but I like it instead of coffee for breakfast.*

19. Not many. *_____ people fully understand Einstein's Theory of Relativity.*

DOWN

1. Covered with liquid; not dry. *Jack fell into the lake and got his clothes all _____.*

3. Things that we eat in order to live. *We were hungry because Mary had not cooked enough _____.*

4. To leave the place where the speaker is. *Let's _____ to the movies this afternoon.*

6. The day after today. *Let's not work any more today. We can finish the job _____.*

7. Pleasing; enjoyable. *The sun is shining and the sky is clear; it's going to be a _____ day.*

8. A printed piece of paper that shows you have paid your fare or admission. *I couldn't get on the bus because I lost my _____.*

10. Moving in the direction of. *He met her while she was walking _____ her car.*

13. Big; more than usual in size or number. *They moved from a small to a _____ apartment.*

18. Preposition, used with a point in time. *Our English class begins _____ 8:00.*

The purpose of these puzzles is to challenge students to write their own definitions for other students to solve. Accurate and legible writing are as important as effective reading. Be sure students understand how to define words before they start the puzzles. If you have not already done so, you may wish to use the suggestions on page 70.

Procedure

a. Divide the class into pairs. Tell them that they are going to make up the definitions for a crossword puzzle and then give that puzzle to their partner to solve.

b. Choose puzzles for the pairs. You may wish to give all pairs the same two puzzles (for example 1A and 1B), or use different puzzles for different pairs. Be sure that each pair has the A and B form of the same puzzle. (There are nine pairs of puzzles, 1A and B through 9A and B.)

c. Distribute the puzzles. Each student gets the blank puzzle form plus the correct answers for it. (You will need to cut apart the answers from your duplicated copies of pages 93 through 95.)

d. Using the right answers, each student writes definitions for his or her puzzle on the blank lines on the puzzle page. Stress to the students that they must write clearly and legibly so that their partner can easily read the definitions.

e. When both partners have completed their definitions, they exchange puzzles. Student A gives his or her puzzle page, with the definitions in place, to Student B, and vice versa. The students *do not* exchange the right answers, however.

f. Using the definitions made up by his or her partner, each student solves the puzzle, writing the words in the diagram at the top of the page. When the puzzles have been completed, the students can check their answers with the original right answers from which the definitions were written.

There is no need for all students to do all nine puzzles, but students will profit from, and will probably enjoy, doing several of them. You might want to give one each day for several days, or two, if there is time and students are still interested.

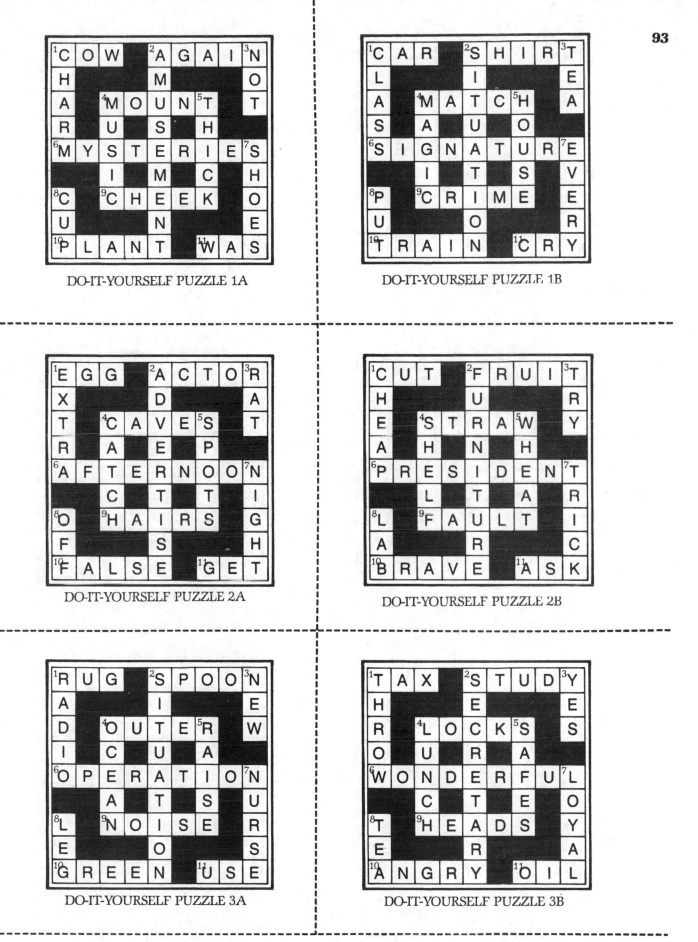

DO-IT-YOURSELF PUZZLE 1A

DO-IT-YOURSELF PUZZLE 1B

DO-IT-YOURSELF PUZZLE 2A

DO-IT-YOURSELF PUZZLE 2B

DO-IT-YOURSELF PUZZLE 3A

DO-IT-YOURSELF PUZZLE 3B

Cut apart on dashed lines and distribute completed puzzles with same-numbered blank puzzle forms.

DO-IT-YOURSELF PUZZLE 4A

```
D I R E C T O R S
I . . . A . . . T
S . C A T C H . R
A . R . . O . . A
P I E . A . M E N
P . A . . E . . G
E . M A R K S . E
A . . . A . . . R
R E L I G I O N S
```

DO-IT-YOURSELF PUZZLE 4B

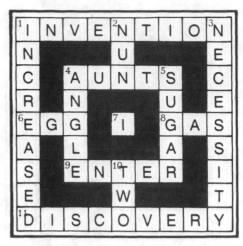

```
I N V E N T I O N
N . . . U . . . E
C . A U N T S . C
R . N . . U . . E
E G G . I . G A S
A . L . . A . . S
S . E N T E R . I
E . . . W . . . T
D I S C O V E R Y
```

DO-IT-YOURSELF PUZZLE 5A

```
E X C E L L E N T
X . . . O . . . E
P . V O W E L . L
E . E . . . I . E
N O R . O . M A P
S . S . . . I . H
I . E V E N T . O
V . . . A . . . N
E X I S T E N C E
```

DO-IT-YOURSELF PUZZLE 5B

```
A D V A N T A G E
P . . . E . . . X
O . T O W E R . P
L . R . . E . . L
O W E . Z . A G O
G . A . . C . . S
I . T E A C H . I
Z . . . I . . . O
E N T E R T A I N
```

DO-IT-YOURSELF PUZZLE 6A

```
S T A T E M E N T
O . . . A . . . R
M . M A R C H . E
E . O . . A . . A
T I N . H . B U S
I . T . . I . . U
M . H E A R T . R
E . . . I . . . E
S U R P R I S E S
```

DO-IT-YOURSELF PUZZLE 6B

```
S C I E N T I S T
T . . . U . . . H
R . W A T E R . E
A . O . . A . . R
N O R . G . I C E
G . S . . I . . F
E . T E S T S . O
R . . . E . . . R
S I G N A T U R E
```

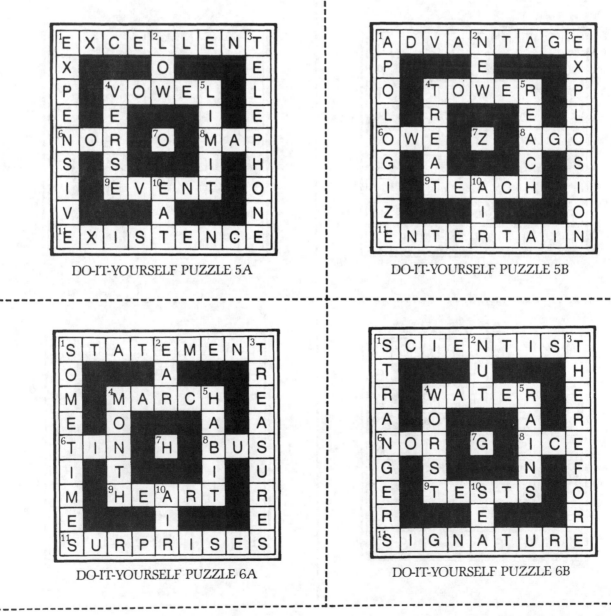

Cut apart on dashed lines and distribute completed puzzles with same-numbered blank puzzle forms.

Talk-A-Tivities©2002 Alta Book Center Publishers, San Francisco, California
Permission granted to photocopy for one teacher's classroom use only.

DO-IT-YOURSELF PUZZLE 7A

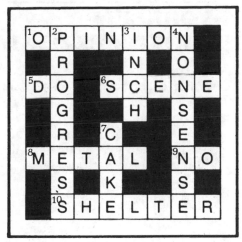

DO-IT-YOURSELF PUZZLE 7B

DO-IT-YOURSELF PUZZLE 8A

DO-IT-YOURSELF PUZZLE 8B

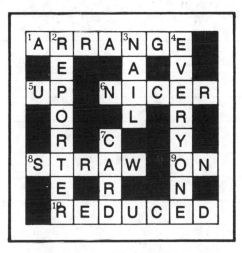

DO-IT-YOURSELF PUZZLE 9A

DO-IT-YOURSELF PUZZLE 9B

Cut apart on dashed lines and distribute completed puzzles with same-numbered blank puzzle forms.

DO-IT-YOURSELF CROSSWORD PUZZLE-1A

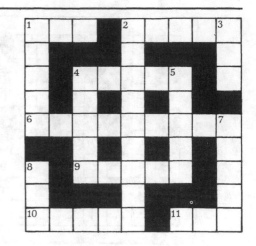

DIRECTIONS. For each word in this puzzle (which you have been given separately), write either a dictionary definition or a defining sentence so that someone else can solve the puzzle. Write clearly so that your handwriting can be read easily. Then give your definitions to a partner, who will try to solve the puzzle.

ACROSS

1. _____

2. _____

4. _____

6. _____

9. _____

10. _____

11. _____

DOWN

1. _____

2. _____

3. _____

4. _____

5. _____

7. _____

8. _____

DO-IT-YOURSELF
CROSSWORD PUZZLE-1B

DIRECTIONS. For each word in this puzzle (which you have been given separately), write either a dictionary definition or a defining sentence so that someone else can solve the puzzle. Write clearly so that your handwriting can be read easily. Then give your definitions to a partner, who will try to solve the puzzle.

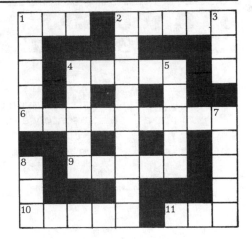

ACROSS

1. _____
_____
_____

2. _____
_____
_____

4. _____
_____
_____

6. _____
_____
_____

9. _____
_____

10. _____
_____

11. _____
_____

DOWN

1. _____
_____
_____

2. _____
_____
_____

3. _____
_____
_____

4. _____
_____
_____

5. _____
_____

7. _____
_____

8. _____
_____

DO-IT-YOURSELF CROSSWORD PUZZLE-2A

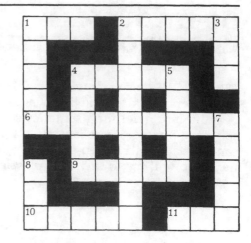

DIRECTIONS. For each word in this puzzle (which you have been given separately), write either a dictionary definition or a defining sentence so that someone else can solve the puzzle. Write clearly so that your handwriting can be read easily. Then give your definitions to a partner, who will try to solve the puzzle.

ACROSS

1. _____
_____
_____

2. _____
_____
_____

4. _____
_____
_____

6. _____
_____
_____

9. _____
_____
_____

10. _____
_____

11. _____
_____
_____

DOWN

1. _____
_____
_____

2. _____
_____
_____

3. _____
_____
_____

4. _____
_____
_____

5. _____
_____
_____

7. _____
_____
_____

8. _____
_____
_____

DO-IT-YOURSELF
CROSSWORD PUZZLE-2B

DIRECTIONS. For each word in this puzzle (which you have been given separately), write either a dictionary definition or a defining sentence so that someone else can solve the puzzle. Write clearly so that your handwriting can be read easily. Then give your definitions to a partner, who will try to solve the puzzle.

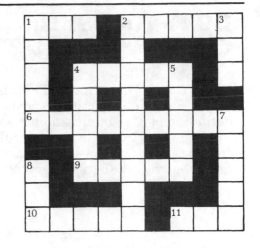

ACROSS

1. _____

_____

_____

2. _____

_____

_____

4. _____

_____

_____

6. _____

_____

_____

9. _____

_____

_____

10. _____

_____

_____

11. _____

_____

_____

DOWN

1. _____

_____

_____

2. _____

_____

_____

3. _____

_____

_____

4. _____

_____

_____

5. _____

_____

_____

7. _____

_____

_____

8. _____

_____

_____

DO-IT-YOURSELF
CROSSWORD PUZZLE-3A

DIRECTIONS. For each word in this puzzle (which you have been given separately), write either a dictionary definition or a defining sentence so that someone else can solve the puzzle. Write clearly so that your handwriting can be read easily. Then give your definitions to a partner, who will try to solve the puzzle.

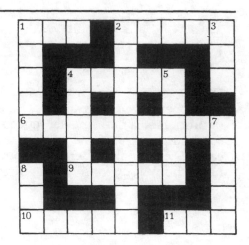

ACROSS

1. _____
_____
_____

2. _____
_____
_____

4. _____
_____
_____

6. _____
_____
_____

9. _____
_____

10. _____
_____

11. _____
_____
_____

DOWN

1. _____
_____
_____

2. _____
_____
_____

3. _____
_____
_____

4. _____
_____
_____

5. _____
_____

7. _____
_____

8. _____
_____
_____

DO-IT-YOURSELF
CROSSWORD PUZZLE-3B

DIRECTIONS. For each word in this puzzle (which you
have been given separately), write either a dictionary
definition or a defining sentence so that someone else can
solve the puzzle. Write clearly so that your handwriting
can be read easily. Then give your definitions to a partner, who will try to solve the puzzle.

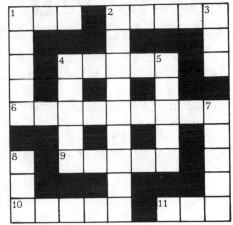

ACROSS

DOWN

1. _____

2. _____

4. _____

6. _____

9. _____

10. _____

11. _____

1. _____

2. _____

3. _____

4. _____

5. _____

7. _____

8. _____

DO-IT-YOURSELF CROSSWORD PUZZLE-4A

DIRECTIONS. For each word in this puzzle (which you have been given separately), write either a dictionary definition or a defining sentence so that someone else can solve the puzzle. Write clearly so that your handwriting can be read easily. Then give your definitions to a partner, who will try to solve the puzzle.

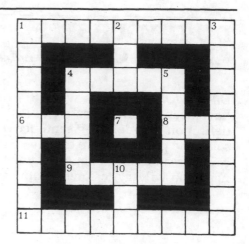

ACROSS	DOWN
1. _____	1. _____
4. _____	2. _____
6. _____	3. _____
7. _____	4. _____
8. _____	5. _____
9. _____	7. _____
11. _____	10. _____

DO-IT-YOURSELF
CROSSWORD PUZZLE-4B

DIRECTIONS. For each word in this puzzle (which you have been given separately), write either a dictionary definition or a defining sentence so that someone else can solve the puzzle. Write clearly so that your handwriting can be read easily. Then give your definitions to a partner, who will try to solve the puzzle.

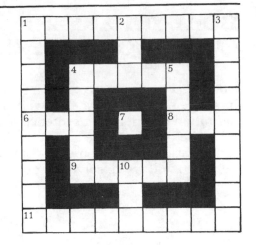

ACROSS

1. _____

_____

_____

4. _____

_____

_____

6. _____

_____

_____

7. _____

_____

_____

8. _____

_____

_____

9. _____

_____

11. _____

_____

_____

DOWN

1. _____

_____

_____

2. _____

_____

_____

3. _____

_____

_____

4. _____

_____

_____

5. _____

_____

_____

7. _____

_____

10. _____

_____

DO-IT-YOURSELF CROSSWORD PUZZLE-5A

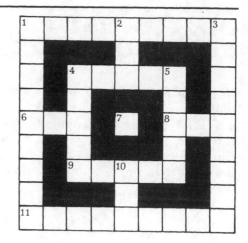

DIRECTIONS. For each word in this puzzle (which you have been given separately), write either a dictionary definition or a defining sentence so that someone else can solve the puzzle. Write clearly so that your handwriting can be read easily. Then give your definitions to a partner, who will try to solve the puzzle.

ACROSS

1. _____

4. _____

6. _____

7. _____

8. _____

9. _____

11. _____

DOWN

1. _____

2. _____

3. _____

4. _____

5. _____

7. _____

10. _____

DO-IT-YOURSELF
CROSSWORD PUZZLE-5B

DIRECTIONS. For each word in this puzzle (which you have been given separately), write either a dictionary definition or a defining sentence so that someone else can solve the puzzle. Write clearly so that your handwriting can be read easily. Then give your definitions to a partner, who will try to solve the puzzle.

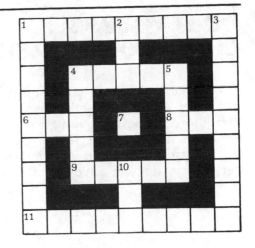

ACROSS

1. _____

_____

_____

4. _____

_____

6. _____

_____

7. _____

_____

8. _____

_____

9. _____

_____

11. _____

_____

_____

DOWN

1. _____

_____

_____

2. _____

_____

3. _____

_____

4. _____

_____

5. _____

_____

7. _____

_____

10. _____

_____

DO-IT-YOURSELF CROSSWORD PUZZLE-6A

DIRECTIONS. For each word in this puzzle (which you have been given separately), write either a dictionary definition or a defining sentence so that someone else can solve the puzzle. Write clearly so that your handwriting can be read easily. Then give your definitions to a partner, who will try to solve the puzzle.

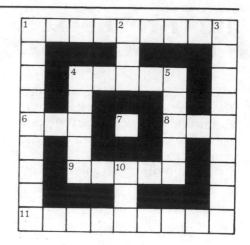

ACROSS

1. _____
   _____
   _____

4. _____
   _____
   _____

6. _____
   _____
   _____

7. _____
   _____
   _____

8. _____
   _____
   _____

9. _____
   _____

11. _____
    _____
    _____

DOWN

1. _____
   _____
   _____

2. _____
   _____
   _____

3. _____
   _____
   _____

4. _____
   _____
   _____

5. _____
   _____

7. _____
   _____
   _____

10. _____
    _____

DO-IT-YOURSELF CROSSWORD PUZZLE-6B

DIRECTIONS. For each word in this puzzle (which you have been given separately), write either a dictionary definition or a defining sentence so that someone else can solve the puzzle. Write clearly so that your handwriting can be read easily. Then give your definitions to a partner, who will try to solve the puzzle.

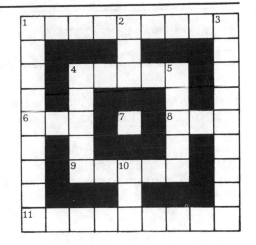

ACROSS

1. _____

4. _____

6. _____

7. _____

8. _____

9. _____

11. _____

DOWN

1. _____

2. _____

3. _____

4. _____

5. _____

7. _____

10. _____

DO-IT-YOURSELF CROSSWORD PUZZLE-7A

DIRECTIONS. For each word in this puzzle (which you have been given separately), write either a dictionary definition or a defining sentence so that someone else can solve the puzzle. Write clearly so that your handwriting can be read easily. Then give your definitions to a partner, who will try to solve the puzzle.

ACROSS

1. _____

5. _____

6. _____

8. _____

9. _____

10. _____

DOWN

2. _____

3. _____

4. _____

7. _____

DO-IT-YOURSELF
CROSSWORD PUZZLE-7B

DIRECTIONS. For each word in this puzzle (which you have been given separately), write either a dictionary definition or a defining sentence so that someone else can solve the puzzle. Write clearly so that your handwriting can be read easily. Then give your definitions to a partner, who will try to solve the puzzle.

ACROSS

1. _____
   _____
   _____

5. _____
   _____
   _____

6. _____
   _____
   _____

8. _____
   _____
   _____

9. _____
   _____

10. _____
    _____
    _____

DOWN

2. _____
   _____
   _____

3. _____
   _____
   _____

4. _____
   _____
   _____

7. _____
   _____
   _____

DO-IT-YOURSELF
CROSSWORD PUZZLE-8A

DIRECTIONS. For each word in this puzzle (which you have been given separately), write either a dictionary definition or a defining sentence so that someone else can solve the puzzle. Write clearly so that your handwriting can be read easily. Then give your definitions to a partner, who will try to solve the puzzle.

ACROSS

1. _____

_____

_____

5. _____

_____

_____

6. _____

_____

_____

8. _____

_____

_____

9. _____

_____

_____

10. _____

_____

_____

DOWN

2. _____

_____

_____

_____

3. _____

_____

_____

4. _____

_____

_____

7. _____

_____

_____

Talk-A-Tivities©2002 Alta Book Center Publishers, San Francisco, California
Permission granted to photocopy for one teacher's classroom use only.

DO-IT-YOURSELF
CROSSWORD PUZZLE-8B

DIRECTIONS. For each word in this puzzle (which you have been given separately), write either a dictionary definition or a defining sentence so that someone else can solve the puzzle. Write clearly so that your handwriting can be read easily. Then give your definitions to a partner, who will try to solve the puzzle.

ACROSS

1. _____

5. _____

6. _____

8. _____

9. _____

10. _____

DOWN

2. _____

3. _____

4. _____

7. _____

DO-IT-YOURSELF CROSSWORD PUZZLE-9A

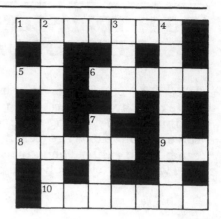

DIRECTIONS. For each word in this puzzle (which you have been given separately), write either a dictionary definition or a defining sentence so that someone else can solve the puzzle. Write clearly so that your handwriting can be read easily. Then give your definitions to a partner, who will try to solve the puzzle.

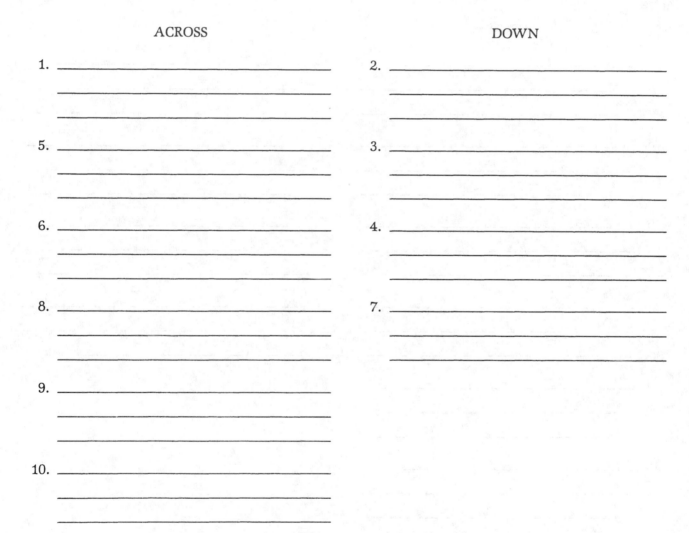

ACROSS

1. _____

5. _____

6. _____

8. _____

9. _____

10. _____

DOWN

2. _____

3. _____

4. _____

7. _____

DO-IT-YOURSELF CROSSWORD PUZZLE-9B

DIRECTIONS. For each word in this puzzle (which you have been given separately), write either a dictionary definition or a defining sentence so that someone else can solve the puzzle. Write clearly so that your handwriting can be read easily. Then give your definitions to a partner, who will try to solve the puzzle.

ACROSS

1. _____

_____

_____

5. _____

_____

_____

6. _____

_____

_____

8. _____

_____

9. _____

_____

_____

10. _____

_____

_____

DOWN

2. _____

_____

_____

3. _____

_____

_____

4. _____

_____

_____

7. _____

_____

_____

This material can be used either as a role-playing activity for two students or as an exercise to practice reading detailed information and filling out an order form. Pages 116 and 117 are selected items from a 1927 mail order catalog, complete with descriptions, specifications, and prices. Page 118 consists of 14 illustrations from the same catalog presented with no names, descriptions, specifications, or prices. The order form on page 115 is adapted from the one in the 1927 catalog.

Procedure

a. Discuss the concept of buying by mail. If possible, bring in and display several current mail order catalogs to establish that people still buy this way. Point out that fifty years ago, many people lived far away from large stores, and the mail order catalog was the only way that they could conveniently buy many things at reasonable prices.

b. Tell the students that you are going to give them two pages from a large mail order catalog published in 1927. They are to imagine that they are living in the United States at that time, more than fifty years ago, and are going to order some things from the catalog.

c. Divide the class into pairs, and give each pair copies of pages 115, 116, and 117. Let them look over the pages carefully. Be sure they understand that these are real items taken from a real catalog of that time. They will find the styles amusing—and the prices startling! Draw attention to the catalog number, size (for many items), and price. You may need to explain these abbreviations: oz. = ounce(s), and lb. = pound(s). Be sure students know that there are 16 ounces in a pound.

d. Then ask one student in each pair to take the two catalog pages and decide on four items to order. The other student (Student B) has the order form and writes down Student A's name and address and the various things that A wants to order, as if taking them down on the telephone. Student A must give the information clearly and completely, and Student B must write it down clearly and completely. After the order form has been filled in, both students should check it for accuracy. Ask them to check especially the catalog numbers, prices, and the arithmetic for figuring the shipping weight and postage.

e. Have partners reverse roles, and have Student B select four other items, while Student A fills out another order form for them.

f. An individual student can also fill out the order form for items of his or her own. Ordering by mail is common enough to make it an important communication skill in itself.

g. Page 118, "Use Your Imagination," can best be done in groups of 3 or 4. Distribute copies of the page and read the instructions (or have them read). After the groups have decided on the names and purposes of the objects, you may wish to tell them what the items, in fact, are (see the Answer Key below).

Answer Key

(1) cement (or feed) mixer; (2) evening bag; (3) churn; (4) fruit press; (5) stationery (letter paper); (6) cream separator; (7) spittoon (cuspidor); (8) camera; (9) steel trap; (10) ornamental fruit bowl (11) white marble figurines; (12) incubator; (13) cornhusker; (14) sewing machine.

ORDER FORM

NAME _____

First Name   Middle Initial   Last Name

STREET _____

CITY _____ STATE _____

Number of article in catalog	Quan-tity	Name of Article	Sizes	Color, Finish etc.	Price for Each	Put total here and add this column	NOTICE: Add weight & figure charges on total weight only.	Weight	
								Lb.	Oz.

PARCEL POST RATES	AMOUNT SENT FOR GOODS		Total
			Lb. Oz.

PARCEL POST RATES

For weights over 8 ounces and up to one pound, the postage is 9¢. For each additional pound or fraction of a pound, add 4¢.

AMOUNT SENT FOR GOODS	
POSTAGE	
TOTAL AMOUNT	

Low Priced — Well Made Sports Wear

"Tom Boy" Knitted Suit

A swagger "Tom Boy" sport suit of fine quality knitted *All Worsted* yarn. Made in clever two-piece style, it consists of a slip-on blouse with a smart woven stripe pattern, while the skirt is of harmonizing solid color. Has attractive adjustable belt, with leather ends and a buckle.

Misses' Sizes—34, 36, 38 and 40 inches bust measure. State size. Shipping weight, 2 pounds.

27H8270—Robinhood Green.
27H8271—Tan. $5.98

27H8270
All Wool Knitted Worsted Two-Piece "TOM-BOY" Sport Suit
$5.98

Coat Style

93c

33K627—Blue with white polka dots. Sizes, 14½ to 17. Half sizes. State size. Shipping weight, ¾ pound.

Our Hercules Triple Stitched Polka Dot Work Shirts. Made coat style of genuine Stifel polka dot shirting. The well known wearing qualities of Stifel cloth, with the practical Hercules features, make a shirt that is hard to excel for both wearing qualities and appearance.

$1.59

38K7602—Navy blue.
38K7604—Maroon.
38K7603—Buff.

Ages, 7 to 14 years. State age size. Shipping weight, 1½ pounds.

A splendid choice in a practical Sweater for the schoolgirl. Knit in a heavyweight from a small amount of wool, balance cotton. Has two pockets and double roll collar that can be buttoned up close around the neck. Well made and will give excellent service. Offered at a reasonable price.

Shpg. wt., 6 oz.

29c

78K6089—Colors: Sand color, bright red, Copenhagen blue or white. State color. Gardenia of genuine leather; also popular coat and dress boutonniere.

Women's and Misses' Sizes

$2.75

Nifty Police Outfit
Police style coat with white braid trimmings on collar and cuffs. Police star and brass buttons. White braid down sides of pants. Good wearing dark blue drill. Leather belt with club and hat with chief's badge.

Sizes, 4 to 14 years. State age size. Shipping weight, 1¾ pounds.

40K3381—Complete Policeman's Suit..............$2.75

27H8250 Corduroy Knickers $2.98

Sturdy and Durable

These good looking knickers are fashioned of strong, sturdy quality *Velour Corduroy*. They have buttoned knee cuffs and an adjustable belt.

Women's and Misses' Regular Sizes—24 to 34 inches waist measure. State exact waist measure. Shipping weight, 2 pounds.

27H8250 $2.98
Tobacco Brown.

Waterproof and Waterproof

Weatherproof and Waterproof

Good grade, attractive and serviceable, gray diagonal surface cotton cloth with heavy blanket lining and an interlining of rubber. Offers absolute protection against rain, wind and cold. To make it more completely a cold weather coat, there is added a warm, heavy beaverized sheepskin collar which turns up snugly about the ears. There are two handy muff pockets and two roomy lower patch pockets with flaps. All around belt with metal buckle. Length, 44 inches. We do not know where else you could secure such thorough protection in such a good looking coat for so little money.

Sizes, 34 to 46 inches chest. State chest measure taken over vest. Shipping weight, 6½ lbs.

41K145—Gray Diagonal Surface Submarine Coat $6.50

78K8470—Fits 22¼ to 23 inches head size.
Colors: Black with Copenhagen blue, or oakwood brown with rose color. Measure and state color. Shipping weight, 2 pounds.

$1.98

Elaborate trimming on a well liked shape and splendid value. Short back poke of good quality silk faced velvet. Brim faced with lustrous **Rayon faille**. Becomingly draped crown. Shaded plush applique set off with stitching. Ribbon crown band and loops at side.

Use Your Imagination

Here are some unusual, old-fashioned items for a farm or household. They are from a 1927 mail order catalog. Choose one object and explain (orally or in writing) what you think it is or what it was used for. Make up a name and purpose; try to persuade your classmates that your idea is correct.

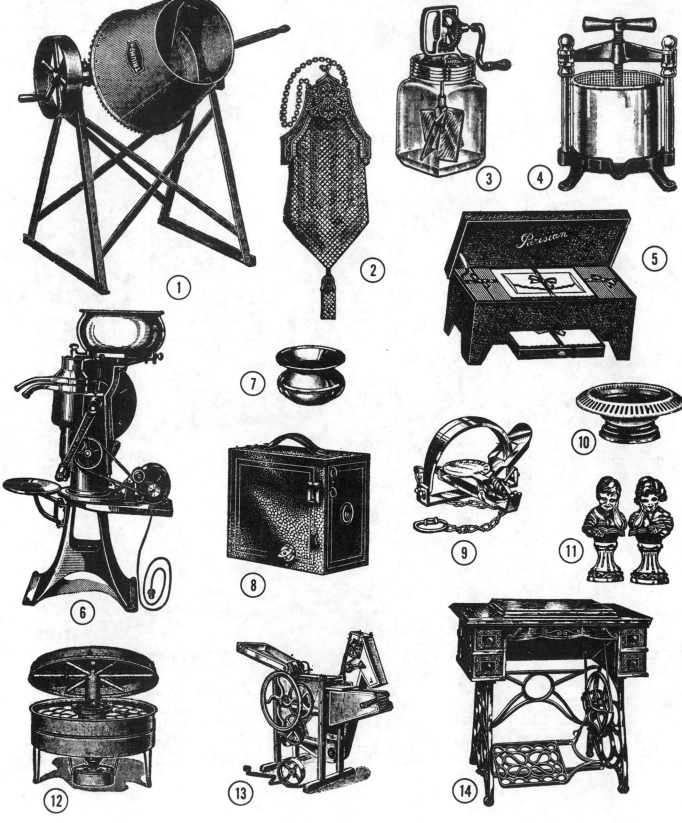

Procedure

a. Give each student copies of pages 120 and 121. Explain that these include material from an actual airline schedule and that they are typical of the way that many airlines set up schedules. Point out, however, that the schedules of particular airlines may differ somewhat in details. For example, they may use different symbols.

b. Be sure students understand "How to Use this Schedule." Using the sample schedule at the top of the left hand column on page 120 (New York to Miami), ask questions that focus attention on the abbreviations and the meanings of each part of the schedule.

c. Have students look at page 121. Make sure they understand that the schedule is organized in terms of the "originating city," the place where the flight starts, and then shows, in alphabetical order, the different destination cities to which one can fly from the originating city, and the schedules to those destinations.

d. Now have individual students practice by doing the six questions at the top of page 120. Provide help if needed.

e. Divide the class into pairs and have them do the six questions at the bottom of page 120.

f. Students may make up other questions to ask, based on the schedule on page 121. In each case, the asking and answering partner should agree on the answer.

To follow up this activity, you may wish to bring in (or have students acquire) timetables of airlines that fly from your city, or that fly to the students' native countries. Using these timetables, students can make up questions for their partners. They may also make up similar questions using cross-country bus schedules or railroad timetables. These follow-up exercises are especially valuable because they focus attention on the similarities and differences between the various timetables or schedules and in so doing foster the development of a "searching behavior" that goes beyond being able to read only one kind of schedule in one particular format.

Answer Key

Page 120, top: (1) Cairo, 2:00 PM; Hong Kong, 8:00 PM; Caracas, 8:00 AM. (2) Flight number 19, leaves 9:00 AM, leaves from JFK International Airport, arrives 11:52 AM, makes no stops, breakfast is served, there is a movie. (3) Same length of time. (4) a. 6:45 PM, b. 11:10 AM, Sunday, c. 1:30 PM, Sunday, d. 12:20, Monday; (5) 2 meals; 1 dinner between New York and San Francisco, and 1 between San Francisco and Honolulu. (6) All flights from Cairo operate only Monday, Thursday, Saturday, and Sunday.

Page 120, bottom: *A to B* (1) 132-4900. (2) Flight number 76/114 leaves at 2:00 PM from O'Hare Airport, arrives at Orly Airport in Paris at 6:55 the next morning (before March 26; it arrives at 7:55 on and after March 26), you change planes at JFK International Airport in New York, leaving there at 6:00 PM, you get two snacks and a dinner, and there are movies on board Flight # 114 between New York and Paris. (3) There are no direct flights to San Francisco from Caracas; you can stop in Los Angeles, in New York, or in San Juan and Miami. *B to A* (1) Narita Airport. (2) You have a choice of three flights, #5 leaving JFK at 10:00 AM and arriving the next day at 9:25 in the evening with one intermediate stop and three meals, lunch, breakfast, and a snack; #15/21 leaving JFK an hour later and arriving the next day at 9:35 in the evening, with a change of plane in Tokyo and three meals, lunch, snack, and dinner, or #801/21, leaving an hour after #15/21, arriving at the same time, and providing the same meal service. All three have movies. (3) This airline has one daily flight from San Francisco to Los Angeles, and one daily flight from Los Angeles to San Francisco. On Tuesday, Thursday, and Sunday, a second flight is available from Los Angeles to San Francisco. Flight time between the two cities is about 1¼ hours.

How to Use this Schedule

	Freq.	Leave	Arrive	Flight No.	Stops or Via	Meals

A ⟍ FROM **New York, NY /**
B ⟍ **Newark, NJ** (EST)

	Reservations	Air Freight
New York	173-4000	132-5800
Newark	124-1300	143-0010

Airports: **K**-JFK Int'l **L**-LaGuardia **E**-Newark

To MIAMI, FL

Freq.		Leave	Arrive	Flight No.	Stops or Via	Meals
ExSu	E	8 30a	11 18a	273	Nonstop	B
Daily	K	9 00a	11 48a	**403**	Nonstop	B
We	E	12 50p	5 41p	361/**63**	TPA	L
Daily	K	1 00p	3 38p	**427**	Nonstop	L
ExSa	K	3 45p	8 21p	218/335	DCA	D
Daily	K	6 15p	9 06p	**453**	1	D
Daily	K	7 15p	8 00a+1	**76**	Nonstop ⊠ DS	
					Above Flt Eff Sep 25	
Daily	K	7 15p	9 00a+1	**76**	Nonstop ⊠ DS	
					Above Flt Dis After Sep 24	

A Originating City

B Airport symbol when more than one airport serves the same city or area.

C Frequency
  Ex = Except
  Mo = Monday
  Tu = Tuesday
  We = Wednesday
  Th = Thursday
  Fr = Friday
  Sa = Saturday
  Su = Sunday

D Destination City

E Departure—Local time.

F Arrival—Local time.

G + 1 = Next day arrival.
  + 2 = Second day arrival.

H Flight number—wide-body aircraft in bold type (See Flight Routing pages for specific equipment on sector).
  Indicates through aircraft with change of flight number.

I Time zone of departure city.

J Passenger or freight reservations telephone numbers in departure city.

K Connecting city (See table below.)
  *Indicates change of airport required.

L Indicates change of plane and flight number.

M Number of intermediate stops.

N In-flight movie.

O Meals. B—Breakfast
  L—Lunch
  D—Dinner
  S—Snack

P Effective or discontinued date of service.

Airport/City Codes

Code	City	Code	City
CAI	Cairo	LGA	New York
CCS	Caracas	LHR	London
DCA	Washington, D.C.	MIA	Miami
EWR	Newark	MNL	Manila
EZE	Buenos Aires	NRT	Tokyo
FCO	Rome	ORD	Chicago
HKG	Hong Kong	ORY	Paris
HNL	Honolulu	SFO	San Francisco
IAD	Washington, D.C.	SHA	Shanghai
IAH	Houston	SIN	Singapore
JFK	New York	SJU	San Juan
LAX	Los Angeles	TPA	Tampa

First take time to study the information at the left and the abbreviated flight schedule of this international airline. Then practice using the schedule on page 121 by answering the following questions.

1. If GMT (Greenwich Mean Time) in London is 12:00 noon, what time is it in Cairo? Hong Kong? Caracas?

2. You are in New York and want to fly to Los Angeles in the morning. What is the flight number? What time does it leave? From what airport? What time does the flight arrive? How many stops does it make? What meals are served? Is a movie shown in flight?

3. Is it faster to fly to Cairo from San Francisco or from Los Angeles?

4. Assume you take flight 22/417 from Tokyo to Caracas on Sunday. What time do you (a) leave Tokyo? (b) arrive in Los Angeles? (c) leave Los Angeles? (d) arrive in Caracas? What day is it when you arrive?

5. If you fly from New York to Honolulu by way of San Francisco, how many meals will be served? When will they be served?

6. What is unusual about the flights from Cairo?

Now work with a partner and ask each other for information about flight schedules.

A ask B

1. What is the telephone number for reservations in Chicago?

2. You are in Chicago and want to fly to Paris. Get as much information as you can about flight number, time of departure and arrival, airport, meals, in-flight movies, etc.

3. Are there direct flights to San Francisco from Caracas? What choice of stops do you have?

B ask A

1. What is the name of the airport in Tokyo?

2. You are in New York and want to fly to Hong Kong on Saturday. Get as much information as you can about flight number, time of departure and arrival, airport, meals, in-flight movies, etc.

3. What flights are there between San Francisco and Los Angeles? What is the flying time between the two cities?

FROM Cairo (GMT +2)

Reservations 747399 | Air Freight 747302

To CARACAS

MoThSaSu	6 40a	9 35p	**111/217**	JFK	✠BLD

To CHICAGO, IL O'Hare Airport

MoThSaSu	6 40a	7 46p	**111/77**	JFK	✠BLD

Above Flt Arrives 8:00p Eff Mar 3

To HONOLULU, HI

MoThSaSu	6 40a	12 25a+1	**111/811**	JFK	✠BLD

To HOUSTON, TX Intercontinental Airport

MoThSaSu	6 40a	8 53p	**111/1**	JFK	✠BLD

To NEW ORLEANS, LA

MoThSaSu	6 40a	7 29p	**111/985**	JFK	✠BLD

To NEW YORK, NY/NEWARK, NJ
Airports: **K**-JFK Int'l **L**-LaGuardia **E**-Newark

MoThSaSu	6 40a	**K**2 15p	**111**	1	✠BLS

To SAN FRANCISCO, CA

MoThSaSu	6 40a	7 30p	**111/855**	JFK	✠BLD

FROM Caracas (GMT −4)

Reservations 284-9211 | Air Freight 284-5411

To CAIRO

TuThFrSa	9 30a	2 30p+1	**218/110**	JFK	✠LDS

To CHICAGO, IL O'Hare Airport

Daily	9 30a	7 46p	**218/77**	JFK	✠LD

Above Flt Arrives 8:00p Eff Mar 1

To HONG KONG

TuFrSu	6 15a	9 35p+1	**418/21**	LAX	✠BLD

To LONDON Heathrow Airport

Daily	9 30a	6 40a+1	**218/2**	JFK	✠LDS

Above Flt Arrives 7:40a Eff Mar 26

To LOS ANGELES, CA

TuFrSu	6 15a	10 05a	**418**	Nonstop	✠BL
Daily	8 15a	5 10p	**442/410**	IAH	✠BLD
Daily	9 30a	6 55p	**218/811**	JFK	✠LD

To NEW YORK, NY/NEWARK, NJ
Airports: **K**-JFK Int'l **L**-LaGuardia **E**-Newark

Daily	8 15a	**L** 4 40p	**442/244**	MIA	✠BS
ily	8 15a	**E** 7 25p	**442/464/**	MIA/	✠BD
.ily	9 30a	**K** 1 05p	**218**	Nonstop	✠L

To PARIS Orly Airport

Daily	9 30a	6 55a+1	**218/114**	JFK	✠LDS

Above Flt Arrives 7:55a Eff Mar 26

To SAN FRANCISCO, CA

TuSu	6 15a	4 15p	**418/120**	LAX	✠BL
Daily	9 30a	7 30p	**218/855**	JFK	✠LD
Daily	11 25a	10 09p	456/495/ 873	SJU/ MIA	✠LSD

To TOKYO Narita Airport

TuFrSu	6 15a	4 20p+1	**418/21**	LAX	✠BLS

FROM Chicago, IL (CST)

O'Hare Airport
Reservations 132-4900 | Air Freight 186-3760

To CAIRO

TuThFrSa	2 00p	2 30p+1	**76/110**	JFK	✠SDL

To HONG KONG

Daily	9 00a	9 25p+1	**561/5**	SFO	✠BLS

Above Flt Eff Mar 2

To LONDON Heathrow Airport

Daily	2 00p	6 40a+1	**76/2**	JFK	✠SDS

Above Flt Arrives 7:40a Eff Mar 26

To NEW YORK, NY/NEWARK, NJ
Airports: **K**-JFK Int'l **L**-LaGuardia **E**-Newark

Daily	2 00p	**K**4 55p	**76**	Nonstop	S

To PARIS Orly Airport

Daily	2 00p	6 55a+1	**76/114**	JFK	✠SDS

Above Flt Arrives 7:55a Eff Mar 26

To TOKYO Narita Airport

Daily	9 00a	4 50p+1	**561/11**	SFO	✠BLD

Above Flt Eff Mar 2

FROM Hong Kong (GMT +8)

Reservations 5-231111 | Air Freight 3-829-8962/3

To CARACAS

WeFrSu	12 35p	12 20a+1	**22/417**	LAX	✠LDS

To CHICAGO, IL O'Hare Airport

Daily	1 30p	7 05p	**6/562**	SFO	✠LSB

Above Flt Eff Mar 1

To HONOLULU, HI

Daily	12 35p	8 25a	**22/830**	NRT	LDS

To HOUSTON, TX Intercontinental Airport

Daily	1 30p	6 10p	**6/12**	SFO	✠LSB

To NEW YORK, NY/NEWARK, NJ
Airports: **K**-JFK Int'l **L**-LaGuardia **E**-Newark

Su	12 35p	**K** 4 50p	**22/16**	NRT	✠LDB
Daily	12 35p	**K** 5 35p	**22/800**	NRT	✠LDB
Daily	1 30p	**K** 7 53p	**6**	1	✠LSB

To RIO DE JANEIRO International Airport

Daily	12 35p	8 10a+1	**22/441**	LAX	✠LDS

To SAN FRANCISCO, CA

Daily	12 35p	10 50a	**22/12**	NRT	✠LDS
Daily	1 30p	9 00a	**6**	Nonstop	✠LSB

To TOKYO Narita Airport

Daily	12 35p	5 15p	**22**	Nonstop	L

FROM London (GMT)

Heathrow Airport
Reservations 409-0688 | Air Freight 759-0094

To CARACAS

Daily	11 00a	9 35p	**101/217**	JFK	✠LSD

To CHICAGO, IL O'Hare Airport

Daily	1 30p	7 46p	**1/77**	JFK	✠LSD

Above Flt Dis After Mar 26
Above Flt Arrives 8:00p Eff Mar 1

Daily	2 30p	8 00p	**1/77**	JFK	✠LSD

Above Flt Eff Mar 27

To HOUSTON, TX Intercontinental Airport

Daily	10 30a	6 55p	**99/925**	MIA	✠LSD

Above Flt Dis After Mar 26

Daily	11 30a	6 55p	**99/925**	MIA	✠LSD

Above Flt Dis After Mar 27

Daily	1 30p	8 53p	**1**	1	✠LSD

Above Flt Departs 2:30p Eff Mar 27

To LOS ANGELES, CA

TuThFrSa	12 15p	3 15p	**121**	Nonstop	✠LS

Above Flt Departs 1:15p Eff Mar 29

MoWeSu	1 45p	6 50p	**121**	1	✠LS

Above Flt Departs 2:45p Eff Mar 27

To NEW YORK, NY/NEWARK, NJ
Airports: **K**-JFK Int'l **L**-LaGuardia **E**-Newark

Daily	11 00a	**K** 1 40p	**101**	Nonstop	✠LS

Above Flt Arrives 12:40p Eff Mar 27

Daily	1 30p	**K** 4 10p	**1**	Nonstop	✠LS

Above Flt Departs 2:30p Eff Mar 27

FROM Los Angeles, CA (PST)

Reservations 170-7301 | Air Freight 146-3884

To CAIRO

TuThFrSa	8 30a	2 30p+1	**72/110**	JFK	✠BDL

To CARACAS

Daily	9 15a	11 35p	**872/498/** 455	MIA/ SJU	✠BDD
Daily	1 00p	4 00a+1	**441/443**	MIA	✠LS

Above Flt Eff Mar 23 thru Apr 8

WeFrSu	1 30p	12 20a+1	**417**	Nonstop	✠LD

To HONG KONG

Daily	12 00n	9 35p+1	**21**	1	✠LSD

To LONDON Heathrow Airport

Daily	8 30a	6 40a+1	**72/2**	JFK	✠BDS

Above Flt Arrives 7:40a Eff Mar 26

MoWeFrSa	2 00p	7 55a+1	**120**	Nonstop	✠DB

Above Flt Arrives 8:55a Eff Mar 26

TuThSu	3 00p	11 30a+1	**120**	1	✠DB

Above Flt Arrives 12:30p Eff Mar 27

To NEW YORK, NY/NEWARK, NJ
Airports: **K**-JFK Int'l **L**-LaGuardia **E**-Newark

Daily	8 30a	**K** 4 31p	**72**	Nonstop	✠B
Daily	12 45p	**K** 8 35p	**20**	Nonstop	✠L

To PARIS Orly Airport

Daily	8 30a	6 55a+1	**72/114**	JFK	✠BDS

Above Flt Arrives 7:55a Eff Mar 26

To SAN FRANCISCO, CA

TuThSu	3 00p	4 15p	**120**	Nonstop	
Daily	9 00p	10 09p	**873**	Nonstop	

To SAN JUAN International Airport

Daily	9 15a	9 33p	**872/498**	MIA	✠BD

To TOKYO Narita Airport

Daily	12 00n	4 20p+1	**21**	Nonstop	✠LSS

FROM New York, NY/ Newark, NJ (EST)

	Reservations	Air Freight
New York	173-4000	132-5800
Newark	124-1300	143-0010

To CAIRO

TuThFrSa	**K** 6 45p	2 30p+1	**110**	1	✠DSL

To CARACAS

Daily	**K** 9 00a	6 00p	**403/445**	MIA	✠BL
Daily	**L**10 00a	6 00p	**241/445**	MIA	✠LL
Daily	**L** 1 00a	11 35p	**353/498/**	MIA/	LDD
Daily	**K** 4 00p	9 35p	**217**	Nonstop	✠D
Daily	**E** 5 15p	4 00a+1	**277/443**	MIA	✠DS

Above Flt Eff Mar 23 thru Apr 8

Daily	**K** 5 30p	4 00a+1	**115/443**	MIA	✠DS

Above Flt Eff Mar 23 thru Apr 8

To HONG KONG

Daily	**K**10 00a	9 25p+1	**5**	1	✠LSD
Sa	**K**11 00a	9 35p+1	**15/21**	NRT	✠LSD
Daily	**K**12 00n	9 35p+1	**801/21**	NRT	✠LSD

To HONOLULU, HI

Daily	**K** 4 00p	12 25a+1	**811**	1	✠DD
Daily	**K** 4 30p	12 07a+1	**855/841**	SFO	✠DD

To HOUSTON, TX Intercontinental Airport

Daily	**K** 8 30a	11 24a	**25**	Nonstop	B
Daily	**K** 3 15p	8 02p	**101/953**	DCA	D
Daily	**K** 6 00p	8 53p	**1**	Nonstop	✠D

To LONDON Heathrow Airport

Daily	**K** 7 00p	6 40a+1	**2**	Nonstop	✠DS

Above Flt Arrives 7:40a Eff Mar 26

Daily	**K** 8 45p	8 25a+1	**102**	Nonstop	✠DS

Above Flt Arrives 9:25a Eff Mar 26

To LOS ANGELES, CA

Daily	**K** 9 00a	11 52a	**19**	Nonstop	✠B
Daily	**K** 4 00p	6 55p	**811**	Nonstop	✠D

To PARIS Orly Airport

Daily	**K** 6 00p	6 55a+1	**114**	Nonstop	✠DS

Above Flt Arrives 7:55a Eff Mar 26

To SAN FRANCISCO, CA

Daily	**K**10 00a	12 59p	**5**	Nonstop	✠L
Daily	**K** 4 30p	7 30p	**855**	Nonstop	✠D

To TOKYO Narita Airport

Sa	**K**11 00a	2 50p+1	**15**	Nonstop	✠LSD
Daily	**K**12 00n	3 50p+1	**801**	Nonstop	✠LSD

FROM Paris (GMT +1) Orly Airport

Reservations 266-4545 | Air Freight 266-4306

To CARACAS

Daily	12 25p	9 35p	**115/217**	JFK	✠LSD

Above Flt Departs 1:25p Eff Mar 27

To CHICAGO, IL O'Hare Airport

Daily	12 25p	7 46p	**115/77**	JFK	✠LSD

Above Flt Dis After Mar 26
Above Flt Arrives 8:00p Eff Mar 1

Daily	1 25p	8 00p	**115/77**	JFK	✠LSD

Above Flt Eff Mar 27

To LOS ANGELES, CA

Daily	12 25p	6 55p	**115/811**	JFK	✠LSD

Above Flt Departs 1:25p Eff Mar 27

To NEW YORK, NY/NEWARK, NJ
Airports: **K**-JFK Int'l **L**-LaGuardia **E**-Newark

Daily	12 25p	**K** 2 30p	**115**	Nonstop	✠LS

Above Flt Arrives 1:25p Eff Mar 26

To SAN FRANCISCO, CA

Daily	12 25p	7 30p	**115/855**	JFK	✠LSD

Above Flt Departs 1:25p Eff Mar 27

FROM San Francisco, CA (PST)

Reservations 197-5200 | Air Freight 177-2525

To CAIRO

TuThFrSa	8 30a	2 30p+1	**201/110**	JFK	✠BDL

To CARACAS

Daily	7 00a	11 35p	**872/498/** 455	MIA/ SJU	✠SBD
WeFrSu	7 00a	12 20a+1	**872/417**	LAX	✠SLD
Daily	12 20p	4 00a+1	**576/443**	MIA	✠LDS

Above Flt Eff Mar 23 thru Apr 8

To CHICAGO, IL O'Hare Airport

Daily	1 15p	7 05p	**562**	Nonstop	L

Above Flt Eff Mar 1

To HONG KONG

Daily	1 00p	9 35p+1	**11/21**	NRT	✠LDD
Daily	2 40p	9 25p+1	**5**	Nonstop	✠LSB

To HONOLULU, HI

Daily	8 45p	12 07a+1	**841**	Nonstop	✠D

To LONDON Heathrow Airport

Daily	8 30a	6 40a+1	**201/2**	**JFK**	✠BDS

Above Flt Arrives 7:40a Eff Mar 26

Daily	11 45a	8 25a+1	**6/102**	JFK	✠LDS

Above Flt Arrives 9:25a Eff Mar 26

WeFr	3 15p	11 20a+1	**124**	1	✠DB

Above Flt Arrives 12:20p Eff Mar 30

TuThSaSu	5 30p	11 30a+1	**124**	Nonstop	✠DB

Above Flt Arrives 12:30p Eff Mar 26

To LOS ANGELES, CA

Daily	7 00a	8 18a	**872**	Nonstop	S

To NEW YORK, NY/NEWARK, NJ
Airports: **K**-JFK Int'l **L**-LaGuardia **E**-Newark

Daily	8 30a	**K** 4 40p	**201**	Nonstop	✠B
Daily	11 45a	**K** 7 53p	**6**	Nonstop	✠L

To PARIS Orly Airport

Daily	8 30a	6 55a+1	**201/114**	**JFK**	✠BDS

Above Flt Arrives 7:55a Eff Mar 26

To TOKYO Narita Airport

Daily	1 00p	4 50p+1	**11**	Nonstop	✠LD

FROM Tokyo (GMT +9)

Narita Airport
Reservations 03-240-8888 | Air Freight 03-240-8841

To CARACAS

WeFrSu	6 45p	12 20a+1	**22/417**	LAX	✠DSL

To CHICAGO, IL O'Hare Airport

Daily	7 00p	7 05p	**12/562**	SFO	✠DSL

Above Flt Eff Mar 1

To HONG KONG

Daily	5 40p	9 35p	**21**	Nonstop	D

To HONOLULU, HI

Daily	9 00p	8 25a	**830**	Nonstop	DS

To HOUSTON, TX Intercontinental Airport

Daily	7 00p	6 10p	**12**	1	✠DSL

To LOS ANGELES, CA

Daily	6 45p	11 10a	**22**	Nonstop	✠DS

To NEW YORK, NY/NEWARK, NJ
Airports: **K**-JFK Int'l **L**-LaGuardia **E**-Newark

Su	6 30p	**K** 4 50p	**16**	Nonstop	✠DB
Daily	7 15p	**K** 5 35p	**800**	Nonstop	✠DB

INDEX

Note: All activities develop speaking and listening skills and the transmission of information from person to person. The listings in this index show some of the particular language and cognitive/interpretive functions emphasized and the specialized vocabulary reinforced.